I'M TRYING TO NUMBER MY DAYS, BUT i KEEP LOSiNG COUNT!

I'M TRYING TO NUMBER MY DAYS, BUT I KEEP LOSING COUNT!

Life Lessons on Living Your Days to the Fullest

Al Sanders

WATERBROOK
PRESS

COLORADO SPRINGS

I'm Trying to Number My Days, But I Keep Losing Count!
Published by WaterBrook Press
5446 North Academy Boulevard, Suite 200
Colorado Springs, Colorado 80918
A division of Bantam Doubleday Dell Publishing Group, Inc.

Scriptures in this book, unless otherwise noted, are from the *New King James Version* (NKJV), copyright © 1979, 1980, 1982, 1992, Thomas Nelson, Inc., publisher. Also cited are: The *Holy Bible, New International Version* (NIV) copyright © 1973, 1978, 1984 International Bible Society, Zondervan Bible Publishers. The *King James Version* of the Bible (KJV). *The Living Bible* (TLB), copyright © 1971 by Tyndale House Publishers, Wheaton, Illinois 60187. Used by permission. *The Message* (MSG). New Testament copyright © 1993. *The Message: The Wisdom Books*, copyright © 1996 by Eugene H. Peterson. All rights reserved. The *New American Standard Bible* (NASB) copyright © 1960, 1962, 1963, 1968, 1971, 1972, 1973, 1975, 1977, 1978 by The Lockman Foundation. Used by permission. The *Holy Bible, New Living Translation,* copyright © 1996. Used by permission of Tyndale House Publishers, Inc., Wheaton, Illinois 60189.

ISBN 1-57856-052-7

Printed in the United States of America
1998—First Edition

10 9 8 7 6 5 4 3 2 1

To Margaret, my wife of fifty years,
and to our family

Contents

Contents

Acknowledgments

TO THE ONE LOVE OF MY LIFE, my wife, Margaret, I'd like to express my appreciation for more than a half-century of marriage and adventure together.

I'd also like to thank our children and their spouses for all they bring to our family: Peggy, Jon, Sharon, Vic, Jim, Robin. And, of course, I could never pass up an opportunity to mention our grandchildren—Heather, Jimmy, Kim, Katherine, Ben, and Kristine—who constantly fill our lives with both joy and blessing.

I owe a debt of gratitude to Evelyn Gibson, who was kind enough—without my knowledge—to submit several short radio scripts to Rebecca Price of WaterBrook Press. This book never would have been born without Rebecca, who, to my amazement, encouraged me to "flesh out" more material for possible publication. I'm grateful, too, for the confidence expressed by Dan Rich, and then the endless hours of "refining fires" in the excellent hands of Nancy Norris and "tweaking" by Sue Ann Jones. What a great team are all these wonderful friends at WaterBrook Press!

Teach us to number our days,
That we may gain a heart of wisdom.

PSALM 90:12

1

Who's Counting?

IT WAS LEATHERY-FACED MOSES who prayed: "So teach us to number our days, that we may apply our hearts unto wisdom" (Psalm 90:12, KJV).

It takes awhile for some of us to learn the lesson Moses taught in the long ago. It's like the old German gentleman remarked: "Ve grow too soon oldt und too late schmart!"

In our younger years, the time so often seemed to pass too slowly as we eagerly counted down the days until Christmas or until school was out and summer vacation started. When I was in college, I would come to work at a clothing store after morning classes and be greeted by a smiling salesman or elevator operator asking, "How many more days, Al?" They were referring to my forthcoming marriage to Margaret. They knew I was eagerly counting the days until our wedding.

When I was in my early sixties, I would endure some sleepless nights (or boring sermons) by eagerly counting the number of days until I reached retirement at age sixty-five. (Now that I've exceeded that mark, I'm not sure I want to retire fully!)

Yes, in the first part of our lives we numbered the days as we waited for something big to happen. And we may have numbered just about everything else, too, including our money, our friends, our possessions—like the rich fool in Jesus' parable:

A rich man had a fertile farm that produced fine crops. In fact, his barns were full to overflowing—he couldn't get everything in. He thought about his problem, and finally exclaimed, "I know—I'll tear down my barns and build bigger ones! Then I'll have room enough. And I'll sit back and say to myself, 'Friend, you have enough stored away for years to come. Now take it easy! Wine, women, and song for you!'"

But God said to him, "Fool! Tonight you die. Then who will get it all?"

Yes, every man is a fool who gets rich on earth but not in heaven. (Luke 12:16-21, TLB)

Like the young fool, we may have surveyed our families, our accomplishments, our possessions—and our days—and said to ourselves, I feel great. I've enough to keep me. Things are going well.

Now, passing life's halfway point, we're growing smarter. Maybe we're finally learning Moses' lesson and seeing that we may be rich on earth—but if we die today who will get it? Now we know the important thing is not whether we're rich on earth but that we are well invested in heaven. And the time may come sooner than we expect when our lives on earth end and God settles our accounts!

Now we grasp the wisdom Moses was asking for, as clarified by The Living Bible's translation of Psalm 90:12: "Teach us to number our days and recognize how few they are; help us to spend them as we should."

You may be wishing, as I do, that Moses had said, "Teach us to number our years" or "months" or at least "weeks." Days seem so transient and fleeting for those of us who've already lived a few thousand of them. They fly by so quickly. How can we ever number them? But God does. He knows the number of days allotted to each of us. He knows when our time will come to meet Him face to face. Right now He's looking down at some of us, knowing when our time on earth will be up. Maybe our days number several more years or only a few more months. Maybe this day will be our last. If you knew this would be your last day on earth, would you be planning your time with more careful thought and deliberation?

The brevity of our lives here on earth is symbolized by a number of fascinating word pictures in Scripture. Here in Psalm 90, Moses said, "We have finished our years like a sigh" (verse 9, NASB). It isn't even a full breath! Psalm 102:3 says, "my days disappear like smoke" (TLB), and Job observed, "My days are swifter than a weaver's shuttle" (7:6, NASB). Every time I read that image I think of my mother, who used to love to do tatting. The strand of thread moved so quickly as she worked it that her fingers were a blur. That's how fast life speeds by.

David looked at his life and prayed, "You have made my days a mere handbreadth; the span of my years is as nothing before you. Each man's life is but a breath" (Psalm 39:5, NIV). How far can you stretch your palm between your thumb and little finger? How long can you make one breath last?

So now, following Moses' advice, we learn to number our days and realize that, whether we live 70 years or 107, they really are few, indeed. How foolish to fritter away our earthly moments as though we were rich with time and had an inexhaustible amount of it available to us! With God's help, we seek to spend each day, each minute, "as we should."

I am attempting to learn to number my days daily, before it's too late, and I'm far from saying that I've mastered the lesson. My constant prayer is, "Lord, help me to end well." With His help, I'll live each day remembering that:

- In the grand race of life, the prize doesn't go to the person who finishes first but rather to the one who finishes well!
- It's faithfulness that counts in the end.
- As someone said, "No thought unworthy of a dying man is ever worthy of a living one."

How many days do I have left? Only God knows. It's not necessary for me to know. Rather, with David, I can say with confidence:

> I bless the holy name of God with all my heart. Yes, I will bless the Lord and not forget the glorious things he does for me.
>
> He forgives all my sins. He heals me. He ransoms me from hell. He surrounds me with lovingkindness and tender mercies. He fills my life with good things! My youth is renewed like the eagle's! He gives justice to all who are treated unfairly....

He is merciful and tender toward those who don't deserve it; he is slow to get angry and full of kindness and love. He never bears a grudge, nor remains angry forever. He has not punished us as we deserve for all our sins.... He is like a father to us, tender and sympathetic to those who reverence him. For he knows we are but dust, and that our days are few and brief, like grass, like flowers, blown by the wind and gone forever.

But the lovingkindness of the Lord is from everlasting to everlasting to those who reverence him....

Let everything everywhere bless the Lord. And how I bless him too! (Psalm 103:1-10,13-17, 22, TLB)

Keep your eyes open for God's providence, keep your heart tuned to sing His praise, and listen to what's taking place around you. The fat lady may not be singing yet—but she's warming up!

2

Warts and All

THE HALL IN OUR HOME is lined with pictures of our family taken over the past several decades. First there's Margaret and me, then come the pictures of our children and grandchildren. The other night I stepped into the hallway and found Margaret looking at a photograph of the two of us that was taken while we were in college.

She turned to me questioningly and asked, "Did we ever look like that—really?"

I stood beside her and stared steadily at the picture of the two young people who smiled back at us with such bright, confident good looks.

"They do look vaguely familiar," I answered.

We looked at that young skin, so smooth without any wrinkles, the hair so thick and dark, those smiles gleaming with confidence and optimism. Oh, to look that young again!

But then I remembered another image: how Margaret had fretted about some minor blemish on her skin. When I looked at her, all I saw was my beautiful fiancée; when she looked in the mirror, all she could see was that tiny little pimple. I wasn't sure my lapels were the right width, and Margaret thought her dress might make her seem old and serious. Looking at that picture fifty years later, we saw a handsome young couple without a single flaw. But fifty years ago, we had looked in a mirror and found lots of imperfections.

We still do. I watch helplessly as my nose seems to get a little bigger each day. And I complain that my knees buckle but my belt won't. Margaret frets about age spots. When we get dressed up and check our mirrored images for slips that show and cowlicks out of control, silent comments flow into our minds: This dress makes me look fat. The lapels on this suit are too narrow (or too wide). My earlobes are getting longer. There's a new wrinkle on my face. I look old!

Apparently we're not alone in this kind of self-criticism. Results of a recent national survey reveal how people can easily become obsessed with their physical appearance:

- Nearly 65 percent would like to change how much they weigh. (Put me in that category! I like that sign someone saw in a doctor's office, posted over the scale. It said, "Pretend it's your IQ.")
- 36 percent of the men would like more hair.
- 34 percent of the women would like better looking legs while about 30 percent were greatly concerned about other parts of their anatomy.
- Both men and women would like to erase obvious telltale facial marks of aging, especially wrinkles.

While most people may be dissatisfied with some aspect of their appearance, by middle age many of us (except those experiencing some kind of midlife crisis that has them running to the plastic surgeon) are learning the truth of that adage claiming real beauty is more than skin deep. We've experienced enough of life to know there is no mirror that can accurately reflect what is in the heart—and that's what really counts.

So, rather than focusing on the mirror, we try to focus instead on the inspired words of the apostle Paul. His strong and certain testimony declared, "I have learned [indicating that the lesson is a continuing process of growth and understanding] in whatever state I am, to be content" (Philippians 4:11).

Here is the beauty of comprehending life's greatest treasures: finding fulfillment and satisfaction with who and what we are, warts and all, imperfections and blemishes included. This kind of self-acceptance brings reward and wealth far greater than the astronomical monetary compensation of CEOs, sports figures, and motion-picture stars.

So we stand before the mirror, and whatever state we are in— skin faded or age-spotted, heads bald or silvered, faces gaunt or wrinkled, chins singular or plural—we thank God! Instead of fretting about the telltale signs that we're growing older, we rejoice in them, remembering Proverbs 20:29, which says a gray head is "splendor," "beauty," "honor," or "glory," depending on which Bible translation you prefer.

It's ironic, I think, that the more we rejoice in whatever shape we're in, the more likely we are to become renewed. It's a trans-formation described in Colossians 3:9-10, which reminds us that, as Christians, we've replaced that same old person staring back at us from the mirror with a new self. And now, just as we've started to think of retirement and being turned out to pasture, we realize we've once again been given a new, ageless life to live, "continually learning more and more of what is right, and trying constantly to be more and more like Christ who created this new life within [us]" (Colossians 3:10, TLB).

Do what you can to stay healthy, and don't fret too much over the thinning hair, thickening waist, increasing wrinkles, or multiplying chins. Rejoice in the new life you've been given—and use it!

3

Immature at Any Age

IT'S AMAZING TO REALIZE how many of us still haven't achieved full maturity—even when we've reached middle-age or "golden years" status! Too often we find ourselves dealing with someone (and if we're honest, we'll have to admit that that "someone" can even be us!) who, despite his or her years, behaves like a child.

Someone told me about encountering such a person on a recent airline flight. It was a woman, quite regal of bearing, who was apparently traveling alone and who found someone else sitting in her assigned seat on the airplane.

"I'm sorry. I know I'm in your seat," the man explained. "But I've just discovered that a close friend from my college days is right here on the other side of the aisle, and I'd appreciate it very much if you would exchange seats with me so we could visit during the flight. We both have connecting flights after this one, so this is our only chance to talk. My seat is just four rows up, and it's on the aisle too. Would you mind?"

The woman glared at the man. "Well, I think everyone should sit in the seat he's assigned," she said icily.

"I'd really appreciate it," the man pleaded.

"You're in my seat, and I'd like to sit there," the woman responded.

As the man collected his belongings and moved to his original seat, the passengers overhearing this conversation must have been reminded of a child who has grabbed a toy from a sibling and fussed, "No! It's mine! I want it! You can't have it!"

As this woman demonstrated, just because we reach a certain age doesn't mean we automatically acquire the corresponding maturity. Instead, we show maturity by the following actions and attitudes:

- Our concern for others outweighs our concern for ourselves.
- The presence of temptation and evil is detected before it becomes sin.
- Irritation is turned aside rather than allowed to develop into full-blown anger and bitterness.
- There is a greater desire to be with God's people in fellowship and worship of the Lord than to use our time on other less-productive pursuits.
- We feel a sincere and eager commitment to grow spiritually.

By the time we've lived four, five, or six decades, we've been through all sorts of ups and downs. If we've learned from those experiences, I'm sure we've also grown a little wiser and gained a little maturity—along with a few pounds, perhaps! On the other hand, if the hard times in our lives have simply piled up on us like a permanent burden we're forced to carry, the opposite can happen. We can grow bitter and self-centered, completely consumed with the difficulties life has dealt us and always anticipating the next wrong that's about to be committed against us.

In contrast, mature Christians look back on their experiences and discover that it was during the hardships that they came to rest more fully on the Lord's promises. They see the good thing that came from the bad. They've matured in their faith, and they know, without a doubt, that God can be trusted to keep His Word.

Last spring a potentially devastating tornado blasted through a bustling downtown area. There was great potential for loss of life, yet amazingly no one was killed by the deadly winds, and only a few people received minor injuries. Why? Because a couple of years earlier, the city had been hit by terrible floods that caused millions of dollars in damage and took several lives—and the city had learned from that experience. City leaders investigated how the lives were lost, found that the warning equipment and procedures were defective, and then installed an updated weather-alert system that allowed government agencies and broadcasters to get the word out quickly, telling residents to take cover immediately. The city had matured; it had learned from its experiences.

In the same way, we mature Christians have learned to use every setback, challenge, and heartache to draw us closer to God so that when the next hard time comes, we turn to Him immediately. Instinctively, we draw strength, courage, and endurance from His powerful presence in our lives. But having once learned that lesson, we don't stop and smugly proclaim ourselves mature disciples, complete in our education. Instead, as Peter urged us, no matter what our calendar age, we continue to "grow in the grace and knowledge of our Lord and Savior Jesus Christ" (2 Peter 3:18, NASB).

Growth is directly tied to grace and knowledge. Grace comes through patiently enduring the testing times the Lord may allow to impact us. Knowledge relates to understanding and applying the truths of His Word.

Have you ever seen an airport in the United States that doesn't have some kind of rebuilding process going on? These travel facilities never seem to be finished; they're always growing and improving. This is exactly what should be true of our lives spiritually. Although we may reach a stage in which we feel confidently mature, we are never finished with the growth or development process until we reach heaven.

Immature people see problems as a frame for their self-centeredness. Mature Christians encounter problems and see opportunities for growth.

4

Defeating Discouragement

PERHAPS YOU HAVE SEEN the little wall plaque that affirms, "Today is the tomorrow you worried about yesterday! And now you know why!" Another dark-humored sage noted, "We're born naked, wet, and hungry—and then things get worse!"

At every age, there are plenty of opportunities to suffer dejection and despair. But if we give in to these emotions, they can sap our mental and moral strength and leave us feeling flat and bitter. We end up with the attitude of the wisecracking actor W. C. Fields, who demanded, "Don't ever call me prejudiced. I hate everybody!"

There is an ancient allegory that tells about Satan's decision to go out of business. He put on sale all his cunning tricks and clever devices, with each destructive tool tagged with a definite price, except for one. Asked why the devil would keep that single specific implement for himself, he replied, "Because through the centuries I've been able to use it to cause the most damage, bringing the defeat and ultimate downfall of scores of Christians!"

And what was that evil weapon, which, by the way, is still an important part of his formidable arsenal? Discouragement.

No matter how old we are, no matter how much we've learned about life, we're all subject to this debilitating problem. Being Christians doesn't automatically make us immune. Jesus warned us we would have problems. He said, "In the world you will have tribulation." But when discouragement threatens to defeat us, we need to remember the rest of Jesus' statement that reminds us we're not left with that tragic fact. The Savior went on to affirm, "But be of good cheer, I have overcome the world" (John 16:33).

My father used to enjoy singing this old chorus that urges us to replace discouragement with joyful trust. It's a favorite of mine too, and I wish I could sing it to you with the proper Scottish "burr," but you'll have to use your imagination:

> Cheer up, ye saints of God,
> There's nothing to worry about,
> Nothing to make you feel afraid,
> Nothing to make you doubt.
> Remember Jesus loves you,
> So why not trust Him and shout?
> You'll be sorry you worried at all
> Tomorrow [roll those Rs!] morning!

Repeatedly the King James Version of the Bible commands us to "be of good cheer" and "be of good courage." Those are the attitudes we need to take when Satan hurls his discouragement weapons our way.

> Be strong and of good courage, do not fear nor be afraid...; for the LORD your God, He is the One who goes with you. He will not leave you nor forsake you. (Deuteronomy 31:6)

5

Gridlock

EACH MORNING I TAKE A MOMENT to look at a special printed chart known as the Amsler grid. If I find that the lines on the chart are straight, I'm reassured about the workings of my eyes. They are affected by macular degeneration and required a troublesome procedure called a vitrectomy a couple of years ago. If the lines are crooked, however, or begin to bend in different places, that means it's time to make another appointment with my ophthalmologist.

The Amsler grid helps me safeguard my vision the same way the Bible helps us safeguard our lives. We hold our thoughts, actions, and opportunities up to God's Word and hope to see them line up straight against the line the Bible cuts through our lives. I like the way the writer to the Hebrews said it: "The word of God is living and active and sharper than any two-edged sword, and piercing as far as the division of soul and spirit, of both joints and marrow, and able to judge the thoughts and intentions of the heart" (4:12, NASB). Applied with discernment, this verse can readily tell us when some parts of our lives are bent, broken, or blurred.

For example, let's look at our priorities as we consider or enter retirement. Let's hold them up against the grid of the Bible and see if the lines are straight. What's your first priority, your chief concern as you enter or live out your retirement? Most of us would have to answer, "Money."

Why is it our bank balance seems to regulate so much of who we are and what we plan to do in life? As the *Wall Street Journal* observed some years ago, "Money is the universal passport to everywhere, except heaven." Certainly money *is* important. At retirement, we know our income will definitely change, and we wonder if we'll have enough money to live out our lives the way we've dreamed.

Retirement brings another overriding concern to many of us. Believing we're sliding down life's slippery slope, we begin to feel continual anxiety over illness (real or imagined) and a foreboding fear of death. Those aches and pains that, in our younger days, wouldn't have caused us a second thought now develop in our minds as full-fledged heart attacks, strokes, or signs of cancer. These concerns have the ability to dog our steps throughout each day, especially when combined with a worry that there won't be enough money in the federal treasury to fully fund programs for Medicare and old-age assistance.

Held up to the Bible's grid, making these two concerns our focus tends to bend our lives out of shape, dent them in toward ourselves when they should be lived straight up against God. When Jesus visited Martha and Mary, Martha's priority was in the kitchen. Mary's was to sit at Jesus' feet. The Lord answered Martha's fussy complaints by saying, "Martha, Martha,...you are worried and upset about many things, but only one thing is needed. Mary has chosen what is better, and it will not be taken away from her" (Luke 10:41-42, NIV).

Jesus is the "one thing" that should be most important to us, no matter what time of life we're in! When He's number one, our other priorities seem to fall into a natural order. When we live our lives for Jesus, we demonstrate a Christlike attitude that rearranges our priorities. One of our foremost concerns becomes a keen interest in living for others. "We aren't here on earth to see through people," as someone has said, "but rather to see people through."

Without this attitude, without the grid of the Bible safeguarding our lives, the danger is that we spend unnecessary time thinking only about ourselves. Such was the case when a woman came to her minister to express her personal concern. "Oh, pastor, I have to confess this terrible sin of pride to someone," she cried. "I don't know what to do!"

He asked her kindly what the trouble was, and the answer astonished him completely. "Why, I just stand in front of the mirror all the time," the woman explained. "I look at myself and say, 'How beautiful you are! How beautiful you are!' Now I need to confess this awful pride."

The response came too quickly as the preacher blurted out, "Ma'am, that isn't pride! That's imagination!"

When we are preoccupied with ourselves, we can come up with some very mistaken ideas!

In Eugene Peterson's refreshing Bible translation, *The Message,* here is how we are encouraged to face life: "Don't push your way to the front; don't sweet-talk your way to the top. Put yourself aside, and help *others* get ahead. Don't be obsessed with getting your own advantage. Forget yourselves long enough to lend a helping hand" (Philippians 2:3-4, emphasis mine).

For me, checking my vision against the Amsler grid each morning is an essential habit. How much more essential should it be for all of us to check our lives against God's Word each day to make sure our priorities align straight and true with the grid of Calvary's cross.

6

Fighting the Fear of Loneliness

I SAW A LIST of what someone called life's worst fears. Not prioritized in any order, the list included such fears as heights, speaking before a group, bridges, dogs, cats, spiders, bugs, snakes, deep water, flying, financial problems, sickness, and death.

Most of the items on the list came as no surprise to me; sometime in my life I'd met someone who had suffered one or more of those fears. I was even familiar with a couple of them myself. Then I noticed the one fear I hadn't expected, hadn't thought of.

The fear of loneliness.

Ah, yes: loneliness. That's a big one, isn't it? Somehow it seems out of place on the list, completely different from those phobias of creepy-crawly things or high places. Perhaps it's because loneliness is a different kind of fear, an intimately personal sense of dread, a secret worry we don't like to admit. But it's certainly a fact of life—especially of long life.

The longer we live, the more friends inevitably pass out of our lives—either because they move away to Sun City or because they fly away to heaven (we hope!). At the same time, as we grow older, it becomes harder to establish meaningful relationships. Making friends seems to take more work than it did in our teenage, college, and young-family years, and some of us just aren't willing to make the effort. Many older people, after the death of their lifelong companion, retreat into sheer reclusiveness. In that state, loneliness may become their constant companion!

So how do we handle this experience that could someday be a reality for all of us? What do we do to prevent or cure loneliness?

First, we grab hold of God's reassuring promise found in Hebrews 13:5 that He will never, never, *never* leave us, and we don't let go. In the longest night, the fiercest storm, the smallest corner, we know He is there. When we keep our sights fixed on the Lord, our problems fade and our loneliness dissipates as His glory lights up the dark places of our lives. It was Helen Lemmel who, in her later years, wrote the familiar lines,

> Turn your eyes upon Jesus,
> Look full in His wonderful face;
> And the things of earth will grow strangely dim,
> In the light of His glory and grace.

That's the first step in dealing with loneliness, turning our eyes away from ourselves and onto Jesus' wonderful face. And then comes step two—and aren't we fortunate to have such a practical solution? Next we simply get out and *do* something beneficial for someone else. Now, of course, for some lonely people this is easier said than done. And the hardest part of all may be getting up out of that recliner and then thinking of some kind deed to do. Maybe, at first, you'll immediately decide to sit back down and make a phone call to brighten someone else's day. Or you might decide to write that note you've been putting off for far too long. If you're really feeling motivated to "take the cure," whip up a

batch of cookies and share them with someone who needs a sweet
little lift. Or pick some flowers and surprise your neighbor.

And always—*always*—offer to pray for the person you're helping (and then *do it*).

When we're battling a case of the lonelies, the crucial point of
this second step is to focus on what we *do* have—family members, friends, acquaintances, neighbors, health, hope, home, or
hamsters—and not to concentrate on who or what we have lost.

After bouts of self-pity, I have discovered that loneliness tends
to disappear when my sights are no longer focused on myself but
on Jesus…and then on others. Helen Lemmel surely knew that
lesson. Although her beautiful poetry proves that she experienced
life from a heavenly perspective, she didn't really *see* anything at
all. She was physically blind! Look at those lyrics again and imagine her choices. She could have sat alone in her dark world,
mourning her loss. Obviously, she made a different choice.

It's amazing, isn't it, when we alter our focus from self to Christ,
how whole new vistas of understanding open up to us?

7

Bonus Years

IT IS AN INCONTROVERTIBLE FACT of life, "Everybody wants to live a long time, but no one wants to get old!"

Just in case you haven't noticed, aging has *always* been a part of the life cycle. This is despite all the appealingly advertised products now on the market and all the advances in cosmetic surgery. We may be able to hide its effects for a while, but there is no human way to slow down, even to the slightest degree, the clock of life. No matter what we do, it keeps on ticking until it stops once and for all.

For most of us, the clock is ticking longer than it did for generations gone by; current statistics clearly indicate that people are living much longer than ever before. If you are twenty-five, you can expect to live five to ten years longer than your grandparents. At the other end of the continuum, if you're already seventy and in reasonably good health, you will probably be here to usher in the new millennium. (I mean the year 2000, not the theologically debated time after the Tribulation.)

While we may celebrate our increasing longevity, we must admit it causes problems for our government. More people are retiring at a younger age. Treasury watchers are telling us that soon there may not be enough people left in the work force to contribute to the pool of financial resources funding the programs for all the retirees. We don't need the politicians to remind us of the obvious problems facing Social Security as well as our country's health-care system struggling to meet the demands of a growing population of older citizens and their attendant maladies.

These facts should make us realize that with our lengthening life spans comes a responsibility. Somehow, through tangible if not monetary means, we need to find ways to be contributors as well as consumers during the last half of our lives. We need to think of ways—as volunteers if not as wage earners—that we can give something back as we come to rely more and more on our government's and society's support in our later years.

But even more important than economic considerations is this vital question we Christians need to face: How can we make whatever time the Lord gives us the most meaningful and beneficial for His kingdom?

First of all, we must simply be aware of this gift of time the Lord has graciously provided to us. Second, whatever our current age, we need to consider how longevity will impact us and our loved ones financially, emotionally, and spiritually.

Then comes the most important requirement: We must practice a solid trust and a strong confidence in God's never-failing promises, remembering that Moses said, "As your days, so shall your strength be" (Deuteronomy 33:25). God isn't going to turn His back on us now, just at the point in life when we may need Him most. This may be the time in our lives when we need to cling to His promises with more determination than ever before.

In the first century A.D., despite impending execution, Polycarp refused to renounce his trust in the Lord. As the torch was about to light the stake to which he was tied, he professed in a strong, clear voice, "I have served Christ these eighty-six years, and He has not injured me once. Shall I now deny Him and lose all hope?"

No matter what happens to us, our responsibility in these "bonus" years is to use them wisely and courageously, always considering whether we're advancing the cause of God's kingdom.

8

Out of the Frying Pan...

RETIREMENT CAN BE THE MOST EXCITING chapter of our lives—or terribly depressing. Most of us look forward to our retirement years as a golden time when we're free to turn off the alarm clock, finally escape the workplace stress we've known so long, and either live a life of leisure or pursue a long-postponed dream. So why does retirement sometimes cause problems? What would have caused the late Erma Bombeck, when her husband retired, to complain, "My life is somewhere to the right of a sedated parakeet."

Most women, especially those who've devoted themselves to full-time homemaking, *do* find that life's dynamics change dramatically when their husbands retire and are suddenly underfoot all day. One woman defined her mate's retirement as "twice as much husband on half as much pay."

In the final analysis, the problem isn't really retirement. It is, rather, the failure to *prepare* adequately for this new adventure. By preparation, I'm not talking about simply following through with a sound financial plan or stashing away funds in your 401(k). There's more to it than making certain your broker is buying when the market is down and selling when it has reached its illusionary peak.

For those of us who are married, when the moment comes for changing work directions and responsibilities, there needs to be a careful balance between the personal goals and desires of both husband and wife. That's what we need to plan and prepare for ahead of time. If we don't, we become vulnerable to the potential for divorce, which can hit a couple most severely during this time of their lives. They may have rocked along fairly successfully for thirty-five or forty years, but without proper preparation they may find themselves retired with few apparent reasons for remaining married. When retirement is begun with advance planning and mutual consideration, both spouses can enjoy a celebration of new and exciting opportunities. As the secular advertisement heralds, "The future belongs to the ones who prepare for it."

One way to prepare is by facing the fact that this stage of life can make us vulnerable to disillusionment and depression. Look at it this way: All our years we have worked and been paid for it. Now, however, we have to expect that there is probably no one who will even ask for, much less welcome, our expertise and opinions. If we haven't been warned to expect this kind of attitude, we may find ourselves mentally pleading, as the psalmist did, "Do not cast me off in the time of old age" (Psalm 71:9).

Anticipating this situation can save a lot of grief and discouragement later. It is good to remember the old axiom that observes, "The second wife *never* calls the first wife to get the husband's favorite spaghetti recipe."

Instead of dwelling on feeling left out and unneeded by our former colleagues, we must forge a new life for ourselves, beginning where we are right now. There are plenty of rewarding jobs for volunteers. If you don't believe it, just check with your pastor or some of the local social-service agencies. Then, as the apostle Paul advised, "Whatever you do, work at it with all your heart, as working for the Lord, not for men" (Colossians 3:23, NIV). As Vance Havner used to say, "I'm not retired—I'm re-fired!"

Now, I must admit, I share this advice about successful retirement as one who has failed at it. Although I often say I'm retired, somehow I manage to come across broadcasting opportunities that continue to hold my interest and keep me working. Maybe I'm just one of those people destined to "wear out instead of rust out," as the saying goes. If so, I consider myself in good company. Right up to the very end, Dwight L. Moody was involved in evangelism. When asked why he maintained such fervor, he affirmed, "I look at this world as a wrecked vessel. One day, God said to me, 'Moody, you're a lifeboat. Go out and rescue as many as you can before the end comes!'"

Would that this same realization could be our earnest desire each day the Lord graciously provides us the opportunity.

9

Stressing the Need to Relax

FOR MANY OF US DRIVEN, TYPE-A PERSONALITIES, one of the hardest things to achieve is genuine relaxation. (By that I mean relaxing and not feeling guilty about it.) Many of us become like out-of-shape rubber bands. We allow stress to stretch our lives until all our resiliency is gone and we're left feeling worn out and used up. We're so accustomed to being constantly pulled in different directions, wound as tight as we can be, that we've forgotten how to be elastic. We can't remember how to relax and enjoy the ebb and flow of life's leisure in between the times when we stretch to meet its pressures and demands. This kind of constant strain and anxiety can cause chronic headaches, high blood pressure, ulcers, heart trouble, and a multitude of other attendant aches and pains (including, from personal experience, insomnia).

There is one very good way to avoid stress-induced problems. This is by allowing ourselves proper leisure. (Please note the emphasis on those two words, *allowing ourselves*.) Often we are our own worst enemies! We give the impression that we are definitely indispensable, that if we can't do it, it won't ever be done right.

Those who live successful lives understand the need for balance between times of stress and times of leisure. They are achievers, but they realize there has to be time to step back, to review and renew commitments, to recharge emotional and spiritual batteries, to examine priorities.

When it comes to this issue of stress, the apostle Paul, without the advantage of a therapist's couch, unquestionably provided the best advice: "Be anxious for nothing, but in everything by prayer and supplication with thanksgiving let your requests be made known to God. And the peace of God, which surpasses all comprehension, shall guard your hearts and minds in Christ Jesus" (Philippians 4:6-7, NASB).

The word *anxiety* carries with it the idea of choking. When we are tense and anxious, we cut off, or suffocate, our lifeline of faith and trust. Letting anxiety and stress dominate our lives is the same as saying we don't believe God can keep His Word.

It would be like going to the post office to mail a letter and then, after using the drop slot, asking the clerk to retrieve the letter we had just mailed. We would have to explain that we've had second thoughts about the ability of the United States Postal Service to do its job adequately! Imagine how God must feel when we treat Him this way!

It's not easy, this idea of relaxing. Ironically, some of us have to work hard at it to do it successfully! This is a favorite conundrum of mine concerning the fruitlessness of filling our minds with fretting: We must work at opening up stress's hard-fisted grip on our lives and then learn to experience real peace instead.

10

Never Too Old

SO WE'RE GETTING ON IN YEARS. And sometimes, if we're honest enough to admit to it, we may be tempted to ponder our experiences and gloat a little bit about the vast storehouse of knowledge we've accumulated. The problem is...we've forgotten where we put the key!

As retirement begins—or continues—many people simply hang up their thinking caps and assume there's nothing else they need to learn. They're happy just to float through the rest of their lives, bobbing along on the surface, learning nothing, contributing nothing. What a shame! The truth is, in the school of life, God's classrooms never close. Every day God gives us the privilege of enrolling in stimulating courses of continuing education. These lessons are sure to bring the wisdom of His infallible Word to each circumstance we encounter as our days fly by.

For example, we honor the Lord by continuing to:

- Learn how to love one another, especially those who may have willfully or unknowingly brought us hurt and embarrassment.
- Learn more about discerning God's will for us. As we start each new day, how much time do we

spend asking the Lord to reveal His perfect plan
to us?

- Learn more about prayer. We should spend less
time reading books about prayer and more time
doing it! Prayer, like oxygen, pumps spiritual blood
and vitality into the brain. And we shouldn't spend
all our time simply repeating our requests. Our
prayer time should include praise too. We shouldn't
be like the little boy who was asked if he prayed
every day. The lad was completely honest and trans-
parent as he responded, "Well, no, not every day.
Some days I don't need anything." Don't forget to
thank God for all your many blessings. As the old
Irish saying urges, "Get down on your knees, and
thank God you're on your feet!"

- Learn from Scripture how to have confidence and
courage. I sometimes sense I am like the man who
explained, "I feel like my life's a spelling bee, and
I've just been given the word:
Supercalifragilistickexpialidoscious!"

- Learn how to number our days. We cannot assume
that we have an unlimited future here on this earth.
No one knows what tomorrow may bring. The
apostle James had it right when he said that our life
is merely a "vapor."

- Learn how to worship the Lord. Too many have the
mistaken idea that worship is simply what we do on
Sunday mornings in church. Worship should be

built into our daily thinking and practice. Just as we express praise or appreciation for a friend or spouse, we need to tell the Lord how much He means to us too! We can never do that too often.

• Learn how to elevate our thinking with the constant realization of the return of the Lord.

Years ago, while I was trying to learn radio electronics at the University of California at Santa Barbara, my friend and professor, who also was an engineer at the radio station where I worked as an announcer, flat-out gave up on me. I hadn't the least bit of interest in Ohms law. In exasperation he promised, "Look, Al. I can see you don't care about learning these things, so tell you what: If you'll just show up each week for the class, I'll give you a passing grade of C."

I sighed, dreading the long, unintelligible class periods to come. Then I put things in perspective and realized how little time the class really would require in comparison to the lifetime I planned to spend in broadcasting. I stuck it out. Looking back, I'm glad I did. Whether or not I intended to, I learned some things from that class. One of the things I learned is that sometimes you learn something simply by showing up! Now, looking back, I can't help but wonder how much *more* I might have gained from that class if I'd put forth just a little more effort.

It's always easier just to show up and bob along. But it's never as rewarding as being involved, especially when the Lord's work is waiting to be done. I have a feeling that *coasting* was not what the apostle Paul had in mind when he wrote, "Therefore, my beloved brethren, be steadfast, immovable, always abounding in the work of the Lord, knowing that your toil is not in vain in the Lord" (1 Corinthians 15:58, NASB).

We've got homework to do!

11

Why Don't We Pray?

MOST CHRISTIANS KNOW there is power, guidance, and strength available through prayer, but many of us would have to admit that our prayer lives are far from what we desire. Why do so few of us, myself included, really take the time to pray as diligently, fervently, and consistently as we should, even when the Scripture clearly instructs us that we "always ought to pray and not lose heart" (Luke 18:1)? Regardless of our age, regardless of our gender, this is Christ's expressed command to us.

Perhaps we simply forget to pray. Or maybe we've become discouraged, realizing it may take years to receive the answers to some of our petitions. It may be that we're discouraged because we've perceived an answer to a particular prayer, and that answer has been no. As the ancient couplet reminds us, "Each prayer is answered, that is so; but for our good, it may be 'No.'"

There are a number of other things that cause us to lose heart. The list includes work pressures, worries about the future, and nagging health problems, not to mention the seemingly hopeless moral situation that surrounds us. We need to be on guard constantly, for there are definite emotional barriers that can hinder our prayers and thus the flow of God's power working through them.

One barrier is our failure to ask according to His will. First John 5:14 says, "Now this is the confidence that we have in Him, that if we ask anything according to His will, He hears us."

Another barrier may be lack of faith. We may ask, but do we really believe it will happen? It's like the man who says, "Well, I don't believe it's possible, but I'll pray for it just the same." I'd rather put my confidence in the prayers of the little girl who attended a church's prayer meeting. The people in that drought-stricken area had met somberly to ask God to send rain. But only the child brought along an umbrella!

Another problem is that many of us don't pray persistently. We give up too soon, forgetting the Lord's parable about the widow who finally won justice after repeatedly appealing to the judge (see Luke 18:3-8) and the apostle Paul's advice to "pray without ceasing" (1 Thessalonians 5:17).

And then there's the barrier of unconfessed sin. Remember how David came to the Lord following his transgression with Bathsheba? He understood the principle as he prayed, "If I regard iniquity in my heart, the Lord will not hear me" (Psalm 66:18, KJV).

These are but a few of the excuses and problems we cite in explaining why we don't pray the way God wants us to. Instead of focusing on our difficulties, however, we should be heartened to consider the powerful results of prayer that are obvious in all walks of life. For instance, we know that prayer breaks down barriers between husbands and wives, children and parents, pastors and congregations, employers and employees. Prayer can melt stony, stubborn hearts (especially our own). Prayer can mend broken and misunderstood relationships.

In prayer we call upon God, the One who never slumbers nor sleeps. Unlike others around us, the Lord doesn't ignore our deepest needs. He is fully aware of the path we're traveling—each stony, thorny step. And best of all, He is never too busy to hear us. We will always be granted His total, undivided attention.

Isn't it sad to realize that in our rushed and stress-filled lives it is far easier for most of us to *talk* about prayer than it is to actually *pray?* The favorite old hymn describes, "Sweet hour of prayer that calls me from a world of care." For many of us it might be more accurate to sing, "Sweet five minutes of prayer"!

Prayer isn't an easy way of getting what we want, but it is the *only* way of becoming what God wants us to be. Charles Spurgeon explained, "Prayer isn't trying to overcome God's reluctance, but instead it is laying hold of His willingness!" The purpose of prayer isn't to change God's mind but rather to make certain our yearnings coincide with His holy purposes. This kind of thinking calls for a genuine assurance of the Lord's ultimate desires for our lives. It is what faith is all about. "And without faith it is impossible to please Him, for he who comes to God must believe that He is, and that He is a rewarder of those who seek Him" (Hebrews 11:6, NASB).

12

Doing Our Duty

I DON'T PRETEND TO UNDERSTAND completely our nation's political processes, but I have tried to vote in almost every election. I feel a need to stay involved, even though I'm sometimes tempted to throw up my hands in disgust and ask myself, "Does my vote really matter?" When that thought comes to me, I consider the following list of close calls in history someone drew up to record when one vote made a difference. For me, such events put an exclamation point on the entire election process.

- In 1645, *one* vote gave Oliver Cromwell control of the British Isles.
- In 1776, *one* vote gave the United States the English language (instead of German)!
- In 1845, *one* vote brought Texas into the Union.
- In 1868, *one* vote saved President Andrew Johnson from impeachment.
- In 1875, *one* vote changed France from a monarchy into a republic.
- In 1876, *one* vote gave Rutherford B. Hayes the presidency.
- And in 1941, *one* vote saved the Selective Service

System from being dismantled, just eleven months before the attack on Pearl Harbor.

It is easy to brush off our personal responsibility and assume there are others who can take up the slack. Too many of us are like the fellow who complained, "The trouble today is that *nobody* is willing to take any responsibility for *anything*. But, please, don't quote me on that!"

Although it is true that we are pilgrims down here and that our permanent citizenship is in heaven, we still have earthly responsibilities. One of them is voting. Remember how Christ set the proper example when it came to paying required taxes to Caesar (see Luke 20:25)?

Whether we're young or old, we need to participate in the selection process of our future leaders. Our votes *do* matter! And once they're elected we have another duty, the biblical mandate to uphold our officials through faithful intercession. We're to pray "for kings and all who are in authority" (1 Timothy 2:2).

Even when we don't agree with our leaders' policies and principles, we can still be effective in interceding for them. That is one of the most beautiful aspects of our relationship to Christ: the gift of the Holy Spirit, who "helps our weakness; for we do not know how to pray as we should, but the Spirit Himself intercedes for us with groanings too deep for words" (Romans 8:26, NASB).

As Christians we are ambassadors for Christ, representatives of heaven. Let us serve our God—and our government—dependably and with devotion.

13

What Really Matters

WHEN I WAS TWENTY-FIVE, I sometimes worried about what people might think of me—not just what they thought of my abilities as a broadcaster, but what they thought about, well, my socks. Or my necktie—was it too wide? Too bold? Too boring? I worried that I'd made grammatical errors. Had I used the proper metaphor? Pronounced that name correctly? Was my speech intelligible and enthusiastic, or was it as dry as old toast? I was convinced it was that indelible first impression that really mattered to people.

But I was wrong!

When I got to be forty-five, I felt much freer to be me. I discovered that it didn't matter nearly as much what other people thought. Not that I allowed myself to be careless in areas of personal grooming or habits of speech. But at middle age, I decided people would just have to accept me as I was. If they had a problem with something I had said or done, it was their business to find a way to deal with the issue. The important thing was that people thought of me as being true to myself, not putting on airs or trying to be something I wasn't.

But I was wrong again!

By the time I got to be sixty-five, my perspective had completely changed again! Finally I comprehended the truth, the stark realization that for all those years, people weren't thinking of me at all!

It's easy to get caught up in believing we have to live our lives according to the current dictates of fashion, morals, and lifestyle, especially in our teenage and young-adult years. After all, it's pretty uncomfortable to be stared at unmercifully by those who obviously perceive us as being ridiculously different or as not fitting in or as being out of touch with reality. But eventually, most of us realize we can't be bound by the pressure to please everyone else. Finally we realize we can never do it. And we see that such concerns over the opinions of others have only resulted in needless self-condemnation.

This isn't to suggest that we suddenly start strolling down the boulevard in our pajamas or disregard all the current customs and courtesies. After all, there is always someone watching—and that person may be changed forever by seeing the reality of Jesus Christ through our words and deeds. The point is, however, and this is the *real* bottom line, that there is actually only One whose opinion ought to matter to us. Obviously our first responsibility is to please God. Scripture reminds us that "all things are naked and open to the eyes of Him to whom we must give account" (Hebrews 4:13). He sees what we wear and what we do, just like everyone else, but He alone knows our every thought and motive. And what *He* thinks of us is the most important thing of all.

We need to be sensitive to the impressions and impact we make on others, of course. That is just a natural part of life. But we don't depend on the world's approval. Our fulfillment comes not from earthly comparisons or compliments but rather from the sufficiency of the Lord. He tells us, "I have loved you with an everlasting love" (Jeremiah 31:3), and we rejoice in His strengthening encouragement. *That's* what really matters.

14

Brain Building

HENRY FORD, WITH HIS CURMUDGEONLY WIT, said, "Make no mistake about it, thinking is hard work. It's no wonder so few people do it anymore!" A similar perspective was shared by one of my favorite country preachers, Vance Havner, who said, in his delightful southern drawl, "So many people are lost in thought these days. And the reason is that it's such unfamiliar territory to them!"

I don't know about you, but for me these little quips aren't as funny as they used to be. It seems that more and more these days I have to depend on constant reminders to accomplish a normal day's agenda—and I have to work to remember where I put the reminders! I'm like the old man who said he was constantly thinking of the hereafter. "I'm forever rummaging around in a drawer or searching through a closet or stepping into a room," he explained, "and suddenly I ask myself, 'What am I *here* after?'"

It seems ironic that I often find myself steadfastly remembering things I wish I could forget while forgetting those things I really want to remember. Sometimes I feel like the fellow who commiserated, "It's hard to feel nostalgic when you can't remember *anything!*"

Although older people are credited with hoarding most of the world's forgetfulness, it's actually common to all of us, regardless of age. Who hasn't frantically flipped through the mental filing cabinet, trying to remember an old friend's name so he or she can be introduced to someone else? It can be someone we've known for years. Yet in that split second, a giant eraser seems to swipe across the slate of our memories, leaving our brains absolutely clean and useless.

The same can be true when trying to remember addresses, birthdays, anniversaries, and other significant events. Just when we need to call them into play, at that very instant it's as if some invisible hand hits the DELETE key on the memory chip of our minds, and we're left remembering the precise date of our first traffic ticket but unable to recall our wedding anniversary.

With varying frequency, this problem happens to all of us at one time or another at every stage of life. But when it happens to us in our later years, it is often accompanied by an alarming question that flashes instantly through our minds: *Could this be the beginning of Alzheimer's?*

I take some degree of comfort in passing what I consider the acid test. It consists of counting backward, without hesitation, from one hundred in increments of seven. This isn't a scientific exercise, but it's a request some physicians make when assessing their patients' mental abilities. You might like to try it, just to prove to yourself you can still do it.

Some people have the erroneous opinion that the human brain is sort of like a chest of drawers with limited capacity. They believe that throughout our lives we put things into its impressive, voluminous drawers. After fifty or sixty years, the drawers begin to bulge and strain to overflowing until eventually the system refuses to accept one more document or piece of information. If a single scintilla of additional data is put into the system, it will automatically crash and cause permanent dementia, they say.

Thankfully there is no evidence that such is the case. As a matter of scientific evidence, the human brain has an *infinite* storage capacity. Unlike even the most sophisticated computer, no matter a person's age, there is still plenty of space left on his mental "hard drive."

But here is what *can* happen—a variation of the "use it or lose it" idea: If there is constant inattention or a lack of the discipline or desire to learn something new or if no real effort is directed toward consistent mental concentration, the mind, like muscles we no longer exercise, begins to atrophy—and eventually shuts down! And once you are over that so-called hill you'll find that you pick up significant speed in forgetting what you truly want to remember.

We can keep our minds in shape through all kinds of activities, hobbies, and volunteer services, depending on our gifts and abilities. The potential for new experiences is limitless. But it's important that we use our minds not only for new experiences but for *worthy* activities. As someone helpfully suggested, we may not be what we think we are, but we *are* what we think. It is as the apostle Paul urged us, "Summing it all up, friends, I'd say you'll do best by filling your minds and meditating on things true, noble, reputable, authentic, compelling, gracious—the best, not the worst; the beautiful, not the ugly; things to praise, not things to curse" (Philippians 4:8, MSG).

15

Maintaining God's Masterpiece

A WOMAN CAME TO THE DOOR of a surgeon's home and rang the bell. A small child, the doctor's four-year-old daughter, answered.

"Is your father home?" the woman sweetly asked.

"Not right now," the little girl replied. "He's performing an appendectomy."

The woman leaned down and condescendingly smiled. "My, that's a mighty big word for a little girl like you. Do you know what it means, dear?"

Whereupon the child brightened and responded quickly, "Sure! It means about three thousand bucks, not counting the anesthesiologist!"

While I have nothing against doctors earning a living, I'd rather not be one of their major sources of financial support! But for many of us, visits to the doctor seem to get more frequent as we age. All of us have favorite "war stories" about these visits, especially about how long we had to wait. One of these days I expect to see the nurse call the name of someone who's been waiting an interminable time in the reception area, only to be told, "Just ask the doctor to have a seat and wait. I'll be with him as soon as I finish reading this article in last year's *Time* magazine."

It's hard to wait, isn't it? While we sit there in the waiting room, reading ancient copies of *Sports Illustrated* and *Working Mother,* we fume to ourselves, thinking our time is just as important as anyone else's, including the physician's. Of course, when we're the cause of the scheduling snafu—either because we called with an emergency or because our routine appointment turned into something more serious—we hope those poor souls out there in the waiting room will be cheerful and patient as they endure the delay!

The aging process brings with it the likelihood that we'll be spending more time in our doctors' offices. After all, what middle-ager hasn't wondered about the possibility of some sudden illness, heart attack, stroke, cancer, Alzheimer's, diabetes, or some other debilitating ailment? While there is always a possibility that one or more of these problems will eventually affect us, we don't need to give such thoughts undue attention. Instead, our focus should be on taking care of ourselves with proper diet and exercise and being encouraged by the constant advances of medical science. For example, problems that only a few years ago required major surgery and several days' hospital stay are now being treated on an outpatient basis using much less invasive procedures. Soon, it is estimated, as many as 25 percent of all surgical procedures may be replaced by other less traumatic methods of treatment.

Should some overwhelming problem eventually confront you or a loved one, one of the best ways to cope is to take action yourself rather than blindly follow whatever is suggested. Begin by asking lots of questions—about the doctor's medical or surgical plan for you, about his or her experience with it, and about alternative possibilities, including "natural" means of regaining your strength and health. Never hesitate to request a second opinion (in fact, some insurance companies require it). And don't worry about hurting the physician's feelings by asking questions. After all, it's your life that's at risk; there is too much at stake for you to hesitate due to shyness or fear of offending.

Gather all the information you can find—from your doctor, from national organizations, from libraries, and from the Internet. Find out which facility has the most successful record in dealing with those suffering from the specific disease or complication you are now experiencing, and if it's feasible, go there for treatment.

The bottom line is to gather information and then to pray, asking also for the prayers of your family and church friends, confidently remembering that your body is the Lord's masterpiece of creation and is "fearfully and wonderfully made" (Psalm 139:14). Thank God for your life and commit it to Him, saying with the psalmist, "My times are in Your hand" (Psalm 31:15).

It is true that as we get older, more of life's chapters seem to end with a question mark than with an exclamation point. But the Lord has brought us this far. You can be sure He will not forsake us now. And in the light of eternity's endlessness, the whole span of our years here is not even measurable on the scale of heaven's incalculable timetable!

16

Loving Again

IT'S TOUGH TO LOSE TREASURED FRIENDS and loved ones to death, especially as we grow older, because the longer we live the more friends we lose. It's tougher still to face the prospect of the death of our mate. Although some of us like to think we might die with our spouses in some common disaster, statistics show that very seldom happens.

Statistics also show that more than 95 percent of the nation's widowed population is now fifty years or older. And by the time a person reaches sixty-five, widows will outnumber widowers five to one! That means, if we didn't know it already, women are generally the surviving spouse (which says something, doesn't it, about their superior physical qualities?).

Whether it's a man or a woman, the surviving spouse usually grapples with questions that are difficult to ask—and to answer. He or she wonders, for example, *Is it possible to love again? Is there someone who would find me attractive and interesting?*

To make decisions on these issues later in life brings in a whole new set of dynamics. If you're a widow or widower who's contemplating a new relationship, it is likely that somewhere down the line you may also find yourself pondering such things as, *What'll my children think?* The *Los Angeles Times* recently reported that cell phones are the latest rage for oldsters who have lost their mates and don't want their children to know about their current activities. (They may have decided to stay out all night with some new friend!) Then you may worry, *What if he (or she) is only interested in my money? What if emotional or health problems develop?*

Then there is the ultimate question: *What about sex?*

The answer seems to be, well, if you're married, of course! In a *Los Angeles Times* article, Dr. Loren Lipson, head of the geriatric division at the University of Southern California School of Medicine, described late-life romances this way: "When you are eighty-five and fall for someone, you act 'goofy' and 'gaga' and hold hands and do the same romantic things you might have done when sixty-five years younger." The truth is that our yearning and churning for companionship never end. So long as we are drawing breath we will have those same biological romantic urges that used to be considered the exclusive domain of young people.

In answering the questions that will inevitably arise, never forget that marriage is first and foremost a divine institution ordained by God Himself. A proposed mate's *spiritual* depth should be the number-one consideration! Be aware that the heart sometimes misreads what is beneath the surface. It believes what it *wants* to believe rather than the actual facts. Although I haven't been through this experience myself, I've been assured by others that this process of discernment can be extremely difficult! The older some people get, the easier it is for them to put on a religious facade. (After all, they have probably had years of continual practice!)

It *is* possible to find a second mate with whom joy can be shared for the rest of life's journey. But without sound judgment coupled with careful and prayerful evaluation, it can also be totally disastrous. Keep in mind that there are circumstances far worse than simply remaining single!

17

New Beginnings

IF YOU HAVE HAD TO ENDURE an unusually high number of trials and testings, if physical illness or emotional pain has been a rather constant companion, you may wonder at times why fate has dealt you such an aggravating set of circumstances. In fact, it is likely that you have even been tempted to think to yourself, and maybe even to express to others, "Life just *isn't* fair!"

That's probably the attitude of the man who moaned: "I lost my car keys at a ball game and never found them. I took the grandchildren to the beach, lost my expensive transition sunglasses, and never found them. I lost my socks in the washing machine and never found them. Then I lost three pounds on a diet, but I found them—PLUS six more pounds!"

The events and issues that sometimes cause us to feel that life isn't fair may be much more serious than the ones recounted in this humorous anecdote. But no matter what causes us to think this way, this is an ideal time to consider making a new beginning. When we begin again, we realize that we can't change the past, but we can certainly ruin a perfectly good future by feeling melancholy and morose about our circumstances.

To begin again, we need to ask the Lord to keep our minds free from the recital of all that is wrong. Otherwise it's possible to repeat the endless details of our tribulations until they become much larger and more formidable than the actual problems. Then when courteous people ask us kindly, "How're you doing?" they're answered with an interminable recitation of all our aches, pains, burdens, and complaints. We have to remember that it just isn't necessary to say something negative every time we're asked!

Once we become open to a new beginning and our minds are freed of the litany of laments, the Lord will give us the ability to see good things in unexpected places. The prophet Isaiah's words are so encouraging in this regard. He urged us, "Forget the former things; do not dwell on the past. See, I am doing a new thing! Now it springs up; do you not perceive it? I am making a way in the desert and streams in the wastelands" (Isaiah 43:18-19, NIV).

The word *desert* here doesn't refer to a resort locale such as beautiful Palm Springs, California. Rather, it describes a place in our lives where we feel barren and burned out. The word *wastelands* symbolizes a time of unhappy experiences, failures, and frustration. When, with God's help, we begin anew, we make our way out of the wastelands of heartache and despair.

It was just such a time during World War II when the people in England were being constantly blitzed by intrusive German buzz bombs. In one particular community, the problems were further complicated by a dwindling water supply; there was very little water for the homes and farms. The people prayed, but things only seemed to get worse. Then one night, a huge bomb exploded in the middle of their area.

"Why would a loving God allow this further injustice?" some wondered. But when the people examined the huge crater the next morning, they discovered to their delight that an artisan well had been uncapped by the blast. Now there was more than ample water for the entire community!

Some of our biggest disappointments are God's greatest triumphs as He brings "streams of living water" from our otherwise dry and parched souls (John 7:38, NIV).

18

Personality Transplant

HAVE YOU HEARD of the cantankerous man whose wife could never seem to please him? No matter how bright and cheery she tried to make each new day's outlook, her husband was always dour and cranky. It is hard to imagine how this gracious woman continued to put up with her crabby mate. But she was determined to make a difference. She worked constantly to make the grouchy man happy and to bring him out of his choleric shell.

One morning she pertly asked, "What can I fix you for breakfast, dear?"

He grumbled with his usual sour-and-sullen disposition, "Gimme two eggs; scramble one, and fry the other sunny-side up."

Humming busily throughout her task, she carefully followed his instructions. Before long she set the attractive plate in front of him. Just as he had ordered, there was a scrambled egg and a fried one, sunny-side up.

But the griper wasn't happy. The wife, completely crestfallen and confused, asked earnestly, "What's wrong? Isn't this what you asked me to fix?"

He complained disapprovingly, "Of course not! You scrambled the wrong egg!"

I hope you don't have to live in such an untenable situation. More importantly, I hope you're not the cause of such a gloom-filled home. Fight the tendency if you must, but don't allow yourself to be a grouch! I so often think of that familiar adage that frequently works in people's lives (I know it is true in mine): You *will* be what you are *now* becoming!

The next time you meet an older person who is a chronic complainer, someone who is obviously not easy to get along with, be careful of your opinion! Please don't ascribe those unpleasant character features as being the result of "the aging process." In all likelihood, that individual began displaying such unfortunate traits when he or she was twenty-five (or even younger). The *person* became the attitude he or she most often showed. You won't find a buoyant, outgoing, agreeable, optimistic, and conscientious thirty-five-year-old eventually turning into a cranky, crabby, critical senior citizen.

Remember: The Lord has placed us here on this earth to represent to others what *spiritual* transformation is all about. While it may not be our job to make people like us, it certainly *is* our primary responsibility, through Christ, to like other people!

Our personalities at thirty are a fairly clear indication of the people we can expect to be three or four decades later. If, in our thirties and forties, we are prone to be angry, short-tempered, irritable, and unhappy, we can count on those same unpleasant personality expressions being exacerbated by the time we reach sixty-five. Let's not kid ourselves! Bitterness soon becomes its own prison where bars on the windows block the light of living and the key for release of the soul has long since been lost. Apart from the transforming power and grace of God, these feelings and emotions are firmly set in concrete long before we reach senior citizenship. Without the Lord's intervention, altering a lifetime personality of anger, selfishness, or bitterness is next to impossible.

If you see yourself in this description, it's time to ask God to help you make some changes in your attitude and personality. You can begin by realizing that, while you may not be able to do a great deal about your current circumstances, you *can* alter your spiritual perception about what God has already done for you.

It reminds me of a classified ad that appeared in a New York City newspaper. The insertion was for an apartment in a run-down tenement district of Manhattan. Knowing the appeal of words, the clever and creative ad writer simply stated,

> For rent: a one-bedroom beauty; has the finest view
> in all of New York City—*if* you look straight up.

That's what a good dose of genuine, Spirit-led optimism can do for you. Don't be consumed by the problems around you. Keep your focus fastened on God, and He will begin a good work in your heart.

The Bible encourages us in making this change, saying, "if anyone is in Christ, he [or she] is a *new* creation" (2 Corinthians 5:17, emphasis mine). This verse assures us there *can* be a radical transformation; there *is* a means, beyond our own human posturing, by which we can start all over again. The same passage goes on to affirm that "all things...become new."

Where we live in central Oregon we are frequently privileged to see beautiful, soaring golden eagles. Naturalists explain that these majestic birds, at various stages in their lives, will grow new beaks. The bird rubs the old beak's superficial crust on a rock until it drops off, revealing the new beak underneath. (Sort of reminds me of my dear mother, who used to say, "I've kept my nose to the grindstone for so long I'm going to have to get a new grindstone!")

The harsh and bitter attitudes that have hardened our hearts for so long are like the eagle's old beak. We rub our lives against the Rock, and the old falls away; the new *us* is revealed. The scope of God's work in us covers personality traits, dispositions, and everything else, and it is an ongoing process, not simply a once-and-for-all transaction. Like the eagle, we may someday find ourselves back at the Rock, painfully rubbing away an old, bitter shell to release the Christlike spirit within us. The theological term for this procedure is *sanctification*. Knowing we can enjoy this kind of power working in our lives each and every day, how can we be anything but joyful?

19

Not So Fast!

AN OLDER WOMAN DRIVING a huge car very cautiously slowed down at a yield sign. The car inched along and finally came to a complete stop. The woman didn't quite seem to know what she should do next. Finally, the impatient and disgusted man behind her, obviously in a hurry, honked, then leaned out the window and shouted, "Hey, lady! It says, 'Yield,' not 'Give up!'"

Next time *you* are tempted to blame someone's erratic driving on his or her old age, it would be a good idea to give the issue a second thought. Duke University recently conducted an interesting survey in which three groups were selected by age categories and tested for driving skills and mental capabilities. The first group consisted of eighteen- and nineteen-year-olds. The next group encompassed a wider age span: from twenty-five to thirty-five. The final group in the driving experiment was comprised of people age sixty-five and older—the age group most often criticized for poor driving habits.

The surprising results showed that the groups performed almost equally in making turns, keeping the car under control at all times, recognizing the various road signs, and stopping the automobile at the right moment and place. The senior category did have decreased peripheral vision, a change that comes with age. And the survey demonstrated that all three groups had the potential for overconfidence that could eventually lead to carelessness. No matter what the age, poor driving habits combined with a lack of concentration cause many accidents.

But here's what is really interesting: Over all, the older drivers scored 15 percent higher than the younger groups! How was this possible? One explanation offered by those conducting the test was that the teenagers tended to drive with only one hand (not with both hands in the traditional "ten-and-two" position on the steering wheel). So maybe we can permit ourselves just a moment of smugness, knowing that our driving abilities, in general, are as good (or better than) drivers of other ages, no matter how many jokes are told at our expense.

It often seems that teenagers are the quickest to make fun of their grandparents' generation, and we older folks are the ones most likely to complain about teenagers' annoying behavior. That's why it's ironic that, when it comes to driving, teenagers find themselves in the same boat with us older drivers: We're *all* targeted for criticism, and a lot of the time it's not merited. (As an interesting aside, statistics show that older people have other problems in common with teenagers. Besides their driving reputations and the age discrimination they face, both demographic groups are largely unemployed, introspective, and frequently depressed. Teenagers and seniors have comparably high suicide rates.)

I like what Paul, inspired by the Holy Spirit, wrote to Timothy: "Don't let anyone put you down because you are young" (1 Timothy 4:12, MSG). He was absolutely right, and I believe we seniors can adapt his advice for ourselves, not letting anyone put us down because we're *old.* Then, together, we can heed what Paul said in the rest of this verse: "Set an example for the believers in speech, in life, in love, in faith and in purity" (NIV). And, I might add, on the road!

20

Renewing Our Youth

IF YOU EVER HEARD me preach, it wouldn't take a great deal of listening to realize I *love* the book of Psalms! I have enjoyed meditating on, studying, and teaching from this 150-chapter book for many years. I especially appreciate the commentary on Psalms compiled by Charles Haddon Spurgeon called *The Treasury of David*. Mine is a well-used three-volume set. You should see all the pages I have carefully marked.

I doubt there is any issue of life that hasn't been powerfully addressed by one of the inspired writers of Psalms. Keep in mind that there were several human authors in addition to David (Moses, Asaph, Solomon; plus numerous chapters bear no direct inscriptions).

Here is one I especially appreciate, now that I'm getting on in years. It is a timely reminder from the 103rd chapter, "Oh my soul, bless GOD, don't forget a single blessing!... He renews your youth—you're always young in his presence" (MSG).

Those four words, "He renews your youth," have always intrigued me. At times I have wondered how one goes about getting back his or her youth. I am sure you would agree, if such a product could be bottled and marketed, it would make the patent holder an instant billionaire. But lacking such a product, how *is* it possible to regain our youth?

Remember this prophetic promise from Isaiah: "Those who wait on the LORD shall renew their strength; they shall mount up with wings like eagles, they shall run and not be weary, they shall walk and not faint" (Isaiah 40:31).

God has something new, exciting, and refreshing for us to experience each day! We can't roll back the actual years, but we can live our lives with renewed strength and soaring spirits when we trust and serve the Lord.

21

Worthless Treasures

RECENTLY A NEWSPAPER ARTICLE caught my eye; it described an elderly woman who had died and left no known relatives. Sometimes these stories have amazing endings. Somewhere in the house—under the mattress, behind the fireplace, or down in the basement behind the furnace—people will find some original stock certificates for Coca-Cola, AT&T, or the Ford Motor Company. Unfortunately, in this case, it wasn't anything like that at all.

When the authorities made a thorough search of this old woman's house, all they found were stacks of newspapers. What could she have possibly seen in those meaningless, outdated publications? Eventually the piles grew so high she made pathways through the veritable forest of folded newsprint. There was literally a wall-to-wall accumulation of *junque* (a higher form of junk) but nothing of value, only debris.

Then the searchers opened a kitchen drawer filled with string. Attached to one small piece was a note that read, "Too short to be of any value." Nearby was a box of miscellaneous buttons with the cryptic marking, "These don't match." In the bathroom, they found several drawers bulging with slivers of soap. Apparently, the woman had never thrown *anything* away.

When I read this story, I realized how so many of us allow our lives to be captivated and cluttered by an accumulation of junk—maybe not to the same extent as this woman but to the extent that our possessions can seem to take priority in our lives.

Jesus said it so well as He observed, "One's life does not consist in the abundance of the things he possesses" (Luke 12:15). Someone else said it this way: The best things in life aren't things!

As valuable as our home, cars, boats, electronics, clothes, and other possessions may be to us now, at Judgment Day such an accumulation will prove to be little more than "wood, hay, and stubble." These earthly treasures will be useless to us when we stand before God and account for our stewardship of the blessings and opportunities He gave us while we lived here.

Corrie ten Boom used to explain, "I have learned how to hold on to things very loosely. The reason for that is because it hurts so much when God has to pry my fingers free."

Look around you. Are you holding your possessions too tightly? Does your lifestyle betray your misguided priorities? Perhaps it's time to start doing more giving than getting. Jim Elliott, the martyred missionary to Ecuador, said it best when he wrote in his diary, "He is no fool who gives what he cannot keep in order to gain that which he cannot lose!"

22

Facing the Future

WHEN MY BROTHER AND I were growing up, there were times when it looked like things that were important to us weren't going to work out the way we wanted them to. Seeing us stew and fret and worry, our mother would offer this familiar sage word of advice: "Whatever will be, will be—even if it never comes to pass."

My mother's advice served me well, but even more preferable is the wise biblical counsel, "No test or temptation that comes your way is beyond the course of what others have had to face. All you need to remember is that God will never let you down; he'll never let you be pushed past your limit; he'll always be there to help you come through it" (1 Corinthians 10:13, MSG).

I learned the King James Version of this verse the night I gave my life to Christ many years ago, and it's been one of my favorites ever since. Thinking of it now reminds me of the story of the small group of Christians who were sharing their favorite scriptures. As always happens, one person came up with John 3:16 (perhaps because it was the only verse he had managed to memorize). Another voted for the shortest verse in the Bible, almost making fun of the poignant words, "Jesus wept" (John 11:35). The best comment in the group, however, was from the man who declared, "Actually, my favorite verse is only a phrase, but it occurs several times in Scripture. It's just five words: 'And it came to pass.'" The words reassured him, he explained, that troubles and trials never come to stay; they "come to pass"!

Whatever you're facing right now, whatever trials may beset you with unremitting and unrelenting torment, be encouraged, knowing that "God will never let you down; he'll never let you be pushed past your limit; he'll always be there to help you come through it." And eventually, this trial will "pass."

Think of David's affirmation when he told the Lord, "Yea, though I walk *through* the valley of the shadow of death, I will fear no evil: for thou art with me" (Psalm 23:4, KJV, emphasis mine). And consider the Father's comforting promises, "When thou passest *through* the waters, I will be with thee; and *through* the rivers, they shall not overflow thee: when thou walkest *through* the fire, thou shalt not be burned; neither shall the flame kindle upon thee. For I am the LORD thy God, the Holy One of Israel, thy Saviour" (Isaiah 43:2-3, KJV, emphasis mine).

The Lord isn't going to leave us in our difficult circumstances. His promise is to take us *through* them! That's all we need to know.

Someone once said that one of the kindest things God has done for us is to put a veil over all our tomorrows. We waste our time and energy when we worry about what lies ahead. Instead, Jesus told us, "Give your entire attention to what God is doing right now, and don't get worked up about what may or may not happen tomorrow" (Matthew 6:34, MSG).

Jesus was a realist. He pointed out that there is sufficient hardship for every twenty-four-hour experience of life. We don't need to worry about our physical, emotional, financial, and relational well-being in the future, because whatever the future brings, God will see us through it *spiritually*. And in the final analysis, this is the dimension of our existence that *really* counts!

Does God care what happens to us? Yes, far more than we could ever imagine. Is He watching over us? Constantly! That was the idea behind the warning sign that appeared at a church youth group's pizza party. Knowing how some teenagers can gorge themselves on this gustatorial delight, someone had wisely made a sign and placed it over the trays of pizza, reminding the young people, "One slice only, please... God is watching."

But you can't outdo resourceful young people. At the other end of the serving line, down where the desserts were spread over the table, another person had creatively hung a placard that read, "Have as many cookies as you'd like; tonight, God is watching the pizza!"

23

Tired of Livin', Scared of Dyin'

THE SIXTH-GRADE SUNDAY SCHOOL class was coming to an end. The earnest teacher had planned her lesson well, and she knew it was time to ask that strategic question. When everyone seemed to be listening intently, she said, "How many of you children would like to go to heaven?"

As you would expect, every hand shot up—except for one boy's. He simply stared at her, remaining passive and indifferent.

The teacher thought she had either failed with the lesson or he hadn't understood the question. With a kind follow-up, she smiled and pressed the inquiry. "Son, don't you want to go to heaven?" she asked.

The boy quickly responded, "Well, sure, I mean, eventually. But the way you put the question, I thought you were makin' up a load right now!"

His answer reminds me of the secular song lyric that describes one who is "tired of living—but scared of dying." Many of us say we want to go to heaven—but we don't want to suffer death to get there! That makes me think, as the old spiritual warned, "Everybody talkin' 'bout heaven ain't a-goin' there!"

While we were on a cruise along the Mississippi River a few years back, my wife and I toured one of the most beautiful homes I have ever seen. It is an antebellum mansion near Biloxi.

Constructed before the Civil War, Longwood Estate is six stories high and encompasses more than thirty-five thousand square feet.

The amazing thing about the mansion is that it has *never* been lived in! It seems the well-intentioned builder went bankrupt before he could finish the structure. Impressive from the outside, today, more than a century later, it still remains an empty shell, only a monument to the lack of proper planning.

When I saw that structure, I was immediately moved by the promise made by Jesus Christ. Just before He left this earth, He assured His followers, "I go to prepare a place for you" (John 14:2).

We don't have to wonder whether Jesus has a well-thought-out plan for how He will fulfill His promise. We don't have to worry that He'll run out of energy or resources before He gets our mansions built. We can depend on His scriptural guarantee. But we have a responsibility, too, to make certain *we* are ready for our mansions! That certainty can only be achieved through personal faith in the Savior.

My wife and I have lived in many houses during our half-century of married life, and some of them have been very special to us. But none of those buildings would have meant nearly so much to us if we had lived in them alone. It was our spouse's presence in the house that really made it special. Similarly, our mansions in heaven will only be glorious because of the presence of our Savior, the Lord Jesus Christ.

When we focus on all the wonderful pleasures we'll enjoy in heaven—face-to-face companionship with Jesus, our beautiful mansions, a glorious eternal life free from pain or sorrow or sickness or fear or death—our eagerness replaces fear.

This poem was read at my father's funeral in 1950. The author and her writing have been favorites ever since.

ALONG THE GOLDEN STREETS

Along the golden streets a stranger walks tonight
With wonder in his heart—faith blossomed into
    sight.
He walks, and stops and stares, and walks and stares
    again;
Vistas of loveliness beyond the dreams of men.
He who was feeble, weak and shackled to a bed
Now climbs eternal hills with light and easy tread.
He has escaped at last the cruel clutch of pain;
His lips shall never taste her bitter cup again.
Oh, never call him dead this buoyant one and free
Whose daily portion is delight and ecstasy.
He bows in speechless joy before the feet of Him
Whom, seeing not, he loved while yet his sight
    was dim.
Along the golden streets no stranger walks tonight;
But one who long home-sick is home at last to stay.
                —Martha Snell Nicholson

Imagine how wonderful heaven will be! Do you want to go there? Are you ready? God is making up a load right now!

24

Feeling Old...and Honored

DO YOU EVER WAKE UP in the morning, get out of bed, look in the mirror, and wonder, *Where did this older person come from?* Feeling old can happen at most any time during life's cycle, whether you're in your thirties or your eighties. But after we pass fifty, we expect that sentiment more and more.

When you were a youngster, if you were like most of us, you probably thought anyone over thirty was old, and someone who had passed his or her fortieth birthday was positively ancient. Isn't it funny how our perspectives change as we add years to our lives?

In our later years, it seems to us that our lives have flown by. Looking back on them, we probably remember celebrating our twenty-first birthdays—and then, the next thing we know, we're staring at that *old* face in the mirror! Such a shock can be hard on our psyches; our first reaction may be to dislike growing old.

But there are several advantages to our seniority, and I'm not just talking about discounts at the car wash and AARP membership. As we age, we gain a special opportunity to serve as Christ's "elder statesmen"—if we keep ourselves properly focused on Him and His kingdom.

I think Paul had this role in mind when he implored us to, "Live in such a way that you are a credit to the Message of Christ"

(Philippians 1:27, MSG). A gracious, kind, and loving older person is a validating proof to the world of God's abundant mercy and abounding grace. By showing this kind of compassion to others, we model for them the kind of God we serve: "compassionate and gracious…, slow to anger, abounding in love and faithfulness" (Psalm 86:15, NIV).

Proverbs calls gray hair "the honor of old men" (20:29, NASB) and "a crown of splendor" (16:31, NIV). So when we look in the mirror and find a gray-haired person staring back at us, instead of being unpleasantly surprised, we should be *honored* to realize we've joined the ranks of God Himself. (After all, He's old too!)

25

A Duty of Love

MANY OF US ARE AT THE AGE when our children are leaving home—and our parents are moving in! Much has been written and broadcast recently about how adult children care for their elderly parents when the parents need continual physical or medical attention. A recent congressional survey put the issue squarely before us and provided some amazing statistics. It showed that, surprisingly, the average couple spends approximately *seventeen* years raising their children. But that same couple can anticipate spending an average of *eighteen* years caring for elderly parents.

This number will continue to rise as the general population lives longer. Medical discoveries, the advent of new and advanced drugs, and early diagnoses are providing the means to alleviate or forestall disabling diseases and to prolong life. Still, old age brings problems, and many families now find themselves trying to cope with an aging parent who is fighting to maintain his or her independence but who obviously needs help and oversight due to mental or physical weakening.

Eventually, the heart-wrenching question confronts the family: "Do we care for Mom (or Dad) in our home, or should some sort of assisted-living facility or nursing home be considered?"

There are no easy answers to this agonizing question. What is true for one family may have absolutely no application to another.

Individual circumstances always make decisions vastly more complicated. The "upside" is that having an elderly parent live with the adult child and his or her family gives the family opportunities to learn invaluable lessons that flow naturally from the parent's many years of life experiences. The downside is that modern families' frenetic schedules and the overemphasis on youth may preclude them from much involvement with the elderly parent.

The advantages of assisted-living facilities are that they afford varying degrees of independence while providing various degrees of care and supervision. They allow seniors to live among those of similar age and provide opportunities for entertainment, education, and sometimes even travel. But finances enter into the equation, of course, and may dictate the ultimate course of action.

Suffice it to say, this discussion is one requiring lots of thought and the involvement of the entire family while remembering our scriptural challenge: "If anyone does not provide for his relatives, and especially for his immediate family, he has denied the faith and is worse than an unbeliever" (1 Timothy 5:8, NIV).

For many adult children already busy with church, family, career, and civic responsibilities, being called upon to care for elderly parents can seem like an overwhelming burden. But keep in mind what an important role our attitudes play in coloring the way we cope with such a challenge. If we think of it as an opportunity to become closer to our parents and as a way to repay them for the years they devoted to us, the job will be easier.

My friend Joni Eareckson Tada has shared something along these lines that has touched me deeply. I appreciate her allowing me to include it here:

Let me describe for you an individual, and, as you hear about him, ask yourself, "Would I be willing to care for this person?"

First, if you walked into this individual's room, it would immediately strike you that he is, for the most part, bedridden and cannot speak (although his caregivers tell you he does recognize some words, and can respond to certain voices). After spending a few moments with this individual, you would see he is unable to walk but can, indeed, sit up.

He cannot feed himself, and so, you would be asked to assist him with his meals. You would have to prepare yourself to feed him slowly since his swallowing capabilities are somewhat limited. This individual also cannot control his bowels or bladder. His sleeping patterns are irregular. At times, for no apparent reason, he reacts violently with frequent loud outbursts.

Is such an individual worth your time and attention? Would you be willing to invest your efforts to assist him with his daily needs? On a scale of one to ten, what value would you ascribe to this person?

Well, before you answer, you should know that this individual is an eight-month-old baby!

What was your attitude as you read through Joni's essay? Did it make a sudden U-turn when you realized her words didn't describe the one you thought they did? Mine did! If our attitudes are "out of alignment," that's the kind of change we need to make so that we graciously and enthusiastically undertake this new role that's opening to us. As our parents' caretakers we must guard against the temptation to judge their value to us simply by their appearance or competence or abilities.

Caring for aging parents may not be easy for us physically, financially, or emotionally. But if we approach the challenge with a gracious attitude and God's help, this time has the potential to become a most rewarding chapter of our lives, bringing us closer to the ones who brought us into this world—and to the One who created us. One person described it most appropriately: "Now my arms hold the one whose arms held me so tenderly for so long—and around us both we feel the mighty arms of God."

When the task seems too great, check your attitude—and remember the words of the psalmist, "GOD is all strength for his people...; Save your people and bless your heritage. Care for them; carry them like a good shepherd" (Psalm 28:8-9, MSG).

26

Living in the Right Dimension

A SIMPLE HALF-HOUR of proper exercise three to five times a week can be a lifesaver—or at least a life-extender, scientists say. It's been proven to reduce cardiovascular problems and to help us maintain our weight and good health. My wife and I love walking together, weather permitting, all seven days of the week. In the resort where we live, we have more than thirty miles of lovely paths, some along the beautiful banks of the Deschutes River. When the asphalt trails are covered with ice and snow, we opt for a few miles on a stationary bike or a few laps around the nearby shopping mall.

While we all know exercise is good for us, it *is* sometimes tempting to postpone or avoid it. As one bumper sticker noted, "To exercise is human—not to is *divine!*" The same is true of going on a diet, which one woman described as "something you keep putting off, while you keep putting on!"

Staying fit and keeping our weight under control take work and willpower, especially as we grow older and our bodies seem to evolve into rounder shapes. As one man complained, "It's hard to feel fit-as-a-fiddle when you're shaped like a cello!" Such frustrations can make us downright petulant, especially if we have friends who seem to stay slim and trim with little effort. One somewhat corpulent woman earnestly prayed, "Oh, Lord, if you won't make me thin, then please let everyone around me look fat!"

Despite the challenges these healthy habits pose, watching what we eat and consistent exercise do pay off in the "end" (and in many other parts of the human anatomy as well!). We just need to *do* it!

One friend said his sixty-five-year-old grandmother took that advice to heart. "About three years ago, she started walking five miles a day," he said. "And now she's walked her way to fitness—unfortunately she's fifteen hundred miles from home!"

That woman who started walking and enjoyed it so much she couldn't stop may have experienced the shift in attitude that is one of the incredible emotional benefits of consistent exercise. As you stick with your program of walking (or whatever exercise you choose to do regularly), your whole outlook on life tends to become brighter. And if you are managing a proper nutritional diet along with the prescribed exercise plan, then weight loss becomes an added benefit. And for most of us, losing weight can produce a rise in personal satisfaction and self-image.

Here's something to keep in mind: Many of the diseases attributed to age are really more related to *inactive* and *immobile* lifestyles! So get out there and get going! As the apostle Paul reminded us, "Didn't you realize that your body is a sacred place, the place of the Holy Spirit? Don't you see that you can't live however you please, squandering what God paid such a high price for" (1 Cornithians 6:19-20, MSG).

Now, admittedly, Paul also said that "bodily exercise profiteth little" (1 Timothy 4:8, KJV), but by that he meant that being fit physically was not to be our primary concern. We must major on the spiritual dimension—as we keep our bodies within healthy dimensions!

27

"But Lord, This Is a *Thorn!*"

ONE OF THE MOST WONDERFUL women I ever met was a gracious and beaming saint. Now with the Lord, Martha Snell Nicholson suffered from rheumatoid arthritis as well as heart trouble, cancer, and rapidly deteriorating sight. I will never forget my privileged visits to her humble residence. She lived in a rather dreary back bedroom of a little home in Wilmington, California, but that little room seemed to glow with her presence. For despite her health problems, she lived joyfully for the Lord.

While I am not usually touched by poetry, this verse, written by Martha Snell Nicholson, has been a favorite of mine for as long as I can remember. It is called "The Thorn."

> I stood, a mendicant of God
> Before His royal throne,
> And begged Him for one priceless gift
> For me to call my own.
> I took the gift from out His hand,
> But as I would depart
> I cried, "But, Lord, this is a thorn,
> And it has pierced my heart!
> "This is a strange and hurtful gift
> Which Thou hast given me."

He said, "Nay, my child, I give good gifts,
And I gave my best to thee."
I took it home, and though at first
The cruel thorn hurt sore,
As long years passed, I grew at last
To love it more and more.
I learned He never gives a thorn
Without this added grace;
He takes the thorn to pin aside
The veil which hides His lovely face.

The apostle Paul understood this "thorn" that Martha Snell Nicholson described so beautifully. Moved by the Holy Spirit, Paul wrote, "Therefore I take pleasure in infirmities, in reproaches, in needs, in persecutions, in distresses, for Christ's sake. For when I am weak, then am I strong" (2 Corinthians 12:10).

As the years gain on us, we often may feel some kind of "thorn" is distracting us, slowing us down, worrying and irritating us. Physical ailments seem to occur more frequently, and chronic health problems that once were only nuisances now threaten to become daily obstacles. As one quipster remarked, this is the time of life when we have "too much room in our houses and not enough room in the medicine cabinet." Doctors' appointments fill our calendars, and various aches and pains tend to dictate our choice of activities.

These thorns could drive us to despair, except for one thing: Jesus. When we are weak, He is strong. When we hurt, He holds us. When we cry out to Him, He answers.

Some writers have compared this stage of life to a desert. They describe it as a time when growth is limited by the harshness of our age and our world. In this desert we tend to focus on ourselves and our current problems rather than on serving others in whatever way is possible for us. We may forget about the glorious future that's waiting for us in heaven. Instead we dwell on each new ache, every additional symptom.

If you find yourself retreating to this kind of hopelessness, realize that the problems you are enduring may be thorns with an added grace. Perhaps now, finally, in your weakness, you will look for Him and understand that "in the desert...God carried you, as a father carries his son" (Deuteronomy 1:31, NIV). And there in the desert, perhaps for the first time, you will find the thorn's gift: a clearer view of God's face.

28

Repeating Parenthood

MOVIE MOGUL SAMUEL GOLDWYN used to say, "Predictions are very difficult to make, especially when they concern the future." If he were still living, I wonder if even Mr. Goldwyn, as farsighted as he was about many public trends, could have predicted what is happening to our families today. For example, could he have imagined the growing population of grandparents now suddenly faced with the task of raising their own grandchildren?

The number of families coping with this generational challenge is ever on the increase. No doubt you know of individuals in this situation in your own neighborhood or church. Millions of children and young people are now living with grandparents who have stepped in to provide a home for the innocent victims of their parents' young age, drug use or other criminal activity, divorce, or death.

For these middle-age and older people, who expected by this time in their lives to be enjoying retirement and the fruits of their labor, everything has suddenly turned upside down. New emotional and physical demands have been thrust upon them as helpless children, who have nowhere else to turn, end up on their grandparents' doorstep!

The emotions of these grandparents run the entire gamut. There is shame, anger, resentment, self-pity, worry over financial needs, and of course, those ubiquitous parental feelings of guilt! Add to this mix their difficulty in understanding and accepting the changing lifestyles and the lack of moral values in today's secular society, and you have the potential for depression and despair.

Should you find yourself in such a difficult position, the best idea is to be absolutely honest with God! Tell Him your feelings, just as the psalmist did, saying, "Thou hast known the troubles of my soul.... Be gracious to me, O LORD, for I am in distress; my eye is wasted away from grief, my soul and my body also. For my life is spent with sorrow, and my years with sighing; my strength has failed...and my body has wasted away" (Psalm 31:7,9-10, NASB). There is no need to hold anything back. After all, He already knows what is going on in your heart and mind.

And when you have purged yourself of all the bitterness, hurt, and bewilderment, keep that channel to God open, because through it will flow the strength and the courage to do what has to be done. Like the apostle Paul, you will find yourself able to "do all things through Him who strengthens [you]" (Philippians 4:13, NASB).

Next, as the saying goes, "put feet to your prayers." Ask your pastor to help you find others in your church or your community who are going through similar situations. A support group can provide encouragement and help in working through tough problems. To be able to talk with others, to compare notes and share ideas and tips, can be a great way for finding encouragement, direction, and eventual hope for the future.

Rearing your grandchildren may be an unexpected and difficult hardship for you, but try to make that fact secondary to the blessings you are providing for the young ones who have been placed in your care. See this new task as one the Lord has selected for you; accept the challenge as surrogate parents to bring stability to the children's lives and provide a godly example for them to follow. As 1 Corinthians 10:31 reminds us, "Whatever you do, do all to the glory of God" (NASB). With that attitude, you will serve as a conduit of the Father's love in nurturing and guiding your grandchildren.

I think of the teacher who took over a sixth-grade class and discovered the school had placed with her a group of kids who really had hope and promise. She excitedly read down the list of names, which were followed by incredible IQ scores, numbers like 113, 126, 134, 141, etc. Because of their intelligence, the teacher treated them with a new and higher degree of respect.

The class grew intellectually under her high-level instruction. It was only at the end of the school year that the teacher discovered these high numbers after the pupils' names were not IQ scores but their locker numbers! She had taught them with an enthusiastic and appreciative attitude, which had brought them encouragement and hope that truly paid off in the way the pupils excelled.

With God as your helper and encourager, there is no limit to the eventual victories and accomplishments you and your grandchildren may experience in the years ahead.

You may feel woefully inadequate for the job. The fact is, you probably are! But just at the point where you need the strength to carry on, the Lord has promised to provide it. Never forget His empowering words: "My grace is sufficient for you" (2 Corinthians 12:9).

As far as the relaxed retirement you had planned to enjoy, I hope you'll find the time you spend with your grandchildren to be far more rewarding—both now and in eternity!

29

Feasting on the Word

I LAUGHED WHEN I HEARD this excellent definition: "Happiness is stepping on the scales the morning after you ate a double portion of lasagna and two pieces of banana cream pie and seeing you didn't gain a single ounce!"

So many of us are warriors in the weight-loss battle. As the years add up, so do the extra pounds. But have you noticed that no matter what we do, most of us end up watching our weight pretty much like we watch our adult children these days? *Helplessly!*

There are some perplexing conundrums when it comes to choosing the right foods. For example, isn't it strange that the same stuff that widens our waists also narrows our arteries? It's hard to know *what* to eat when one day the news tells us a particular food promotes health and increases longevity, and the next day we find it's blamed for cancer and ulcers! Such confusion makes me think of the comedian (I think it was Milton Berle) who said, "I stopped eating 'natural foods' when I discovered 80 percent of all deaths are due to natural causes!"

Obviously, I find it much more fun to joke about dieting than to actually do it. For instance, I love the list a friend of mine sent me that enumerates various exceptions to traditional dieting rules. It says that food has no calories if no one sees you eat it and that drinking a diet soda cancels out the calories of the candy bar you eat at the same time! My favorite item on the list says that the calories in food used for medicinal purposes (hot chocolate, cheesecake, milkshakes, and lasagna) *never* count.

Although it's fun to laugh about the need to watch our weight, it's also important to take seriously the fact that, as believers, we're to maintain our bodies as sanctified dwelling places of God's Holy Spirit. Thus, we must be aware that what we eat is critically important to our future health and to our ability to be of service to the Lord.

Sometimes overeating isn't just an indulgence. Very often cravings for food are due to underlying psychological reasons such as loneliness, low self-esteem, guilt, and even childhood sexual abuse. Any of these triggers can be the hidden force causing the extra, unnecessary pounds to add up. In such cases, only God can provide the ultimate strength that empowers us to exert our human willpower and defeat the problem.

When you're finally tired of all the jokes and you're ready to get serious about caring for your body, God's temple, as you should, consider Paul's reminder in 1 Corinthians 6. I like the way *The Message* paraphrases the familiar words: "You know the old saying, 'First you eat to live, and then you live to eat?' Well, it may be true that the body is only a temporary thing, but that's no excuse for stuffing your body with food.... Since the Master honors you with a body, honor him with your body."

Pleasing the Lord is a powerful impetus to make changes. Instead of opening the refrigerator, try opening the Bible when you feel yourself yielding to food's temptations. Instead of overeating, feast on His Word. It can guide you to physical as well as spiritual triumph.

Go for it!

30

Just Imagine...

ONE OF THE GREATEST PRIVILEGES my wife and I enjoy is spending time with our grandchildren. Living so far away from the six of them makes their visits cherished and more memorable. It is fun to talk with them and to hear their outlooks on life. Sometimes their perspectives help us look at our own world a whole new way.

For example, Heather, our oldest granddaughter, was utterly amazed when she discovered her grandmother and I lived before there was television. "Grandpa, if you only had radio, what did you look at; what did you watch?" she asked incredulously.

That made me stop for a few moments, reflecting. Then I told Heather about the wonderful way those old radio dramas and comedy shows had caused us to use our imagination. With my mind's eye, I explained to Heather, I could clearly "see" what was happening, even though they were only being described with audible words. I saw the scenes as I *imagined* them—probably far more intricately than any set designer could have created or any photojournalist could have captured on video (and all this with absolutely *no* expense for the producer!).

Remembering the vivid details of those imagined scenes and the thrilling excitement of the narrators' stories reinforced a medical study that was mentioned recently in the news. It refuted the old maxim credited to Confucius that "a picture is worth a thousand words." Instead, the medical studies showed the mind can retain what it *hears* five times longer than what it *sees*. A good example of that is the fact that we don't know what Confucius looked like, but we *do* remember his words!

As Heather and I talked about my generation's "deprived" childhood, I began thinking of some of the other things our grandchildren take for granted that weren't even imagined when I was a child: minivans, computers and e-mail, Post-it notes, cellular phones, handheld global-positioning satellite systems that show you *exactly* where you are on earth, fax machines (even in your car!), video cameras and VCRs, CDs (both bank deposits and compact discs), "insider trading," Visa and MasterCard (how could we possibly have existed without them?), call waiting (along with call forwarding and caller ID), remote controls (we had to actually get up and change the radio dial), AIDS, sushi (maybe they had it, but it is not something our parents ever made us eat), Trivial Pursuit, shopping malls, jet skis, televangelism... Listening to my list, Heather's eyes grew large. Now *she* was having to use her imagination, trying to picture living without some of these everyday inventions.

Afterward, I kept thinking about how our world has changed and realized that, when we get right down to the bare essentials, we now have plenty of things to live *with*, but I really question whether we have more things to live *for!* New products and discoveries seem to burst into our world every day, but they soon sink into tedious mediocrity, and like Heather, we find ourselves taking for granting the things that once were mind-boggling. Someone has observed that "a 'wonder' grows gray-headed in seven days." (That may have been the same person who observed that "the best things in life aren't *things!*")

Then I remembered that, through all the changes in all the generations in all the centuries, one thing has remained *un*changed: the Father's love for us. He is *always* faithful to each one of His children. He will *never* change. He is "the same yesterday, today, and forever" (Hebrews 13:8). Yet His presence never grows "gray-headed" and monotonous. Just imagine it! His mercies "are *new* every morning" (Lamentations 3:23, emphasis added), yet He is the one constant that never changes.

31

The Journey Is the Joy

A LITTLE BOY WATCHED as his mother filled out a visitors' card at church. At the bottom, there were places to indicate the generational category that most closely fit the person's age. When he saw where she had checked, the boy exclaimed in astonishment, "Mommy, you're in the next-to-last box!"

Someone has said, "Life can only be understood backwards, while it *must* be lived forward." Before we know it, we've passed through life's entire check list, and there we are, in the next-to-last box, finally understanding what we see as we look backward through the years. Sometimes it's only from that perspective that we realize the fortune in family, health, or friendship we failed to appreciate while we were actually living it! Mark Twain must have been looking back from that vantage point when he supposedly said, "Youth is such a wonderful time of life; it's a shame it's virtually wasted on the young!"

When we're young, we're eager to be eighteen so we can be considered an adult. Then we can't wait until we're twenty-one and have full rights of adulthood. Next, perhaps, we're eager for our wedding day or for college graduation or for the birth of our child. So much of our lives is spent anticipating the future that we don't always stop to fully enjoy the *now*. Suddenly we find ourselves contemplating retirement and wondering, *Where did the time go?*

Now, in our later years, we understand what Job meant when he said, "My time is short—what's left of my life races off too fast for me to even glimpse the good. My life is going fast, like a ship under full sail, like an eagle plummeting to its prey" (9:25-26, MSG).

It was at bedtime when a little girl knelt to say her nightly prayers and got her words turned around as she recited the well-known rhyme. Without realizing it, she said, "If I wake before I die…"

Perhaps that's what some of us should be praying every day—that we finally wake up and realize we're still in the land of the living. In fact, Scripture calls us to rouse out of lethargy and inactivity when it says:

> So how long are you going to laze around doing
> nothing?
>   How long before you get out of bed?
> A nap here, a nap there, a day off here, a day off there,
>   sit back, take it easy—do you know what comes
>   next?
> Just this: You can look forward to a dirt-poor life,
>   poverty your permanent houseguest!
>   (Proverbs 6:9-11, MSG)

Old age isn't a disease! Retirement isn't a time to stop *living*. It is simply another exciting chapter of that which commenced at conception. It is another phase in our God-given life cycle in which we can honor and serve our Creator!

This is the ideal place to share one of my favorite gems about our attitude toward life:

> Tucked away in our subconscious mind is an idyllic vision in which we see ourselves on a long journey that spans an entire continent. We are traveling by train and, from the windows, we drink in the passing scene of cars on nearby highways, of children waving at crossings, of cattle grazing in distant pastures, of smoke pouring from power plants, of row upon row of cotton and corn and wheat, of flatlands and valleys, of city skylines and village halls.
>
> But uppermost in our minds is our final destination—for at a certain hour and on a given day, our train will finally pull into the station with bells ringing, flags waving, and bands playing. And once that day comes, so many wonderful dreams will come true. So restlessly, we pace the aisles and count the miles, peering ahead, waiting, waiting, waiting for the station.
>
> "Yes, when we reach the station, that will be it!" we promise ourselves. "When we're eighteen...win that promotion...put the last kid through college...buy that 450 SL Mercedes Benz...pay off the mortgage...have a nest egg for retirement..."
>
> From that day on we will all live happily ever after.
>
> Sooner or later, however, we must realize there is no station in this life, no one earthly place to arrive at

once and for all. The journey is the joy. The station is an illusion—it constantly outdistances us.

Yesterday's a memory, tomorrow's a dream. Yesterday belongs to history, tomorrow belongs to God. Yesterday's a fading sunset, tomorrow's a faint sunrise. Only today is there light enough to love and live.

So, gently close the door on yesterday and throw the key away. It isn't the burdens of today that drive men mad but rather the regret over yesterday and the fear of tomorrow.

"Relish the moment," is a good motto [especially when coupled with Psalm 118:24: "This is the day which the LORD hath made; we will rejoice and be glad in it"]. So stop pacing the aisles and counting the miles. Instead, swim more rivers, climb more mountains, kiss more babies, count more stars. Laugh more and cry less. Go barefoot oftener. Eat more ice cream. Ride more merry-go-rounds. Watch more sunsets. Life must be lived as we go along.[1]

1. Robert Hastings, "The Station," *A Penny's Worth of Minced Ham* (Carbondale, Ill.: Southern Illinois University Press, 1986). Used by permission of Mrs. Robert Hastings.

32

Pass It On

A BUMPER STICKER EMBELLISHED the back chrome bumper on one of those high-priced, tanklike motor homes. As the metal behemoth tooled down the highway, I couldn't help but smile when I read the words, "We're spending our children's inheritance!"

While most of us have probably seen that same bumper sticker on vehicles ranging from rattletraps to Rolls-Royces and understand the humor behind those sentiments, we look to the Bible, rather than to highway humor, for instructions about caring for the needs of our own families. As Paul instructed Timothy, "If anyone does not provide for his own, and especially for those of his household, he has denied the faith and is worse than an unbeliever" (1 Timothy 5:8).

In providing for our own, we first need to look carefully at the kind of legacy we will be leaving our children and grandchildren. When most of us think of inheritance, we think of material goods. But Christians know there is a far more important legacy we must pass on to our children and grandchildren. There is no higher calling than a positive and consistent spiritual witness lived out steadily and dependably day by day. We can be certain that others are observing our lifestyles. What they learn from us is our legacy to them.

Beyond the spiritual inheritance, there is also the need for wise and prayerfully planned stewardship spelled out in a proper will. This should be a rewarding testimony of our personal faith in Christ, but it should be drafted with care—and with the advice of legal counsel, if needed. It's important that we make certain our desires and provisions are clearly defined and adequately expressed in proper court-approved "legalese."

Some years ago my wife and I inquired about and found a trusted attorney who specialized in this field of service. We had him prepare what is known as a "revocable living trust," a legal device in which we placed all our earthly possessions so that our estate will not be taxed to oblivion upon our demise. We had the living trust established about a dozen years ago and recently updated it to reflect our new address, our additional grand-children, and the organizations we want to remember with our final financial stewardship.

If we've worked hard, saved carefully, and been good stewards of our earthly blessings, it may be tempting, in our comfortable state, to flatter ourselves as we survey our accumulated treasures. We may even start imagining that our homes or whatever busi-nesses or property we may have developed have become a kind of monument to ourselves. The psalmist described that attitude this way: "Their inner thought is, that their houses are forever, and their dwelling places to all generations; they have called their lands after their own names" (Psalm 49:11, NASB).

But again and again the Bible reminds us to keep our earthly riches in perspective. "Do not be overawed when a man grows rich, when the splendor of his house increases," the psalmist continued. "For he will take nothing with him when he dies, his splendor will not descend with him" (49:16-17, NIV).

The good thing about drawing up a will or a trust is that it helps us realize we're not taking anything with us. One of these days we'll leave everything behind without even a backward glance. Remembering this fact and knowing we've provided for our loved ones, we can then turn our focus to more important matters: living each day for the One who provided our possessions in the first place!

33

Are We Living Yet?

GROWING OLDER CAN BE DEPRESSING—or it can mean we've reached the best time of our lives. For the most part, the choice is ours.

Moses said, "We have finished our years like a sigh" (Psalm 90:9, NASB). That sounds peaceful enough, but whenever I read that verse, I remember visiting the hospital bedside of the first person whose death I ever witnessed. Her final moments came with just a sigh. It's a sound I'll never forget.

Instead of living these later years "like a sigh" I'd probably tend more toward poet Dylan Thomas's attitude that "Old sage should burn and rave at close of day." I don't think God intended that we should simply fade away, our lives dwindling down to nothing. Instead, I believe He wants us to burn with zeal for Him and to rave about the wonders of His creation right up to the day He calls us home.

Philosopher Robert Nozick wrote recently, "Our senior years free us to act in a more dramatic and risky fashion than younger, more prudent folks would ever venture. Those of us blessed to endure to this point have a chance of defining ourselves anew. Seizing an adventure to advance the cause of truth, goodness, beauty or holiness, provides a way, in the latter part of our lives, to shine most brightly."

Think of the adventures seized by the former American president who, in his seventies, enjoyed skydiving for the first time; the eighty-year-old great-grandmother who took her first ride on a Harley-Davidson (traveling the same speed as her age); and the woman who fulfilled her hidden goal of bungee-jumping at the age of ninety-one! Life is all about taking risks while enjoying God's bounteous blessings along the way. In our later years, we have more freedom, more flexibility, to shine in ways we may never have dreamed of before—or, conversely, that we've dreamed of for decades and been unable to attempt!

Granted, skydiving, motorcycle-riding, and bungee-jumping are a little too risky for some of us, but there are plenty of other, less terrifying ways we can live to the fullest this life we've been given.

Choosing how we can "shine most brightly" is different for each of us. Determining the adventurous ways we will serve God with enthusiasm and devotion in the last half of our lives can involve some exciting choices. Will we tutor a child, teach an immigrant to read, build a house for the homeless, or deliver food to the elderly and housebound? Will we volunteer to guide the startup of a young entrepreneur's fledgling business, teach a Sunday school class, organize a Bible study, or serve as a guide at the local museum?

Whatever "adventures" we choose, it's important to choose *something*. We shouldn't give up living just because we're growing older. God never tells us to settle back in our rocking chairs and wait for the undertaker to prepare our bodies for the "Uppertaker." (My spell-checker couldn't find that one!) We are meant to capture a dynamic and fulfilling vision for the future.

I think of the man who, after many years of travel, returned to his hometown. There he inquired about some of his former friends. About one of them, he asked, "Is Jones yet living?"

He received the interesting reply, "No, not yet!"

We must ask ourselves often, "Am I living?" And we must strive to answer *Yes!*

34

Give, Give, Give!

EXPLAINING WHY HE SELDOM attended church, one man said, "All I ever hear about when I go to church is money. The preacher constantly talks about finances. His theme is, 'Give, Give, Give!'"

When you stop to consider the core of the gospel message, "Give, give, give!" isn't a bad summary at all. In fact, the more I think about it, the more I realize it's actually a great definition of our Christian faith and the Christian way of life! We are urged to give, that's true. But we're taught to give much more than just money; we're to give our talents, our energies, our devotion. And to demonstrate this lesson to us, we have as our role model God, who gave His only begotten Son, and we have the Son Himself, who gave everything for us—even His life! No matter what our financial status is, and no matter how much we give, we can *never* outgive God!

Admittedly, talking about giving makes a lot of people nervous; they squirm uncomfortably on the Sundays when the preacher's subject is stewardship—the way we handle the funds and the other blessings the Lord has graciously entrusted to us. And no wonder so many people don't like to hear this message! An intriguing item on the television news recently described a survey indicating that the average person gives *less* than 1 percent of his or her income to charitable causes, including local church or parachurch organizations as well as the Red Cross, Boy Scouts, American Cancer Society, Easter Seals, Alzheimer's Foundation, and any number of other worthy causes.

Despite our nation's affluence, the survey said, those dedicated souls who do invest in helping others typically give less than 2 percent of their income. (Incidentally, during the Great Depression, that average was more than 3 percent!) It is a sad fact that many people will give less to God than they will add as a tip for their meal. The Bible recognizes the importance of the tithe (10 percent) and assures us that additional offerings, given in faith and love, will also be blessed.

Sometimes we hear church leaders urging us to give, and we find ourselves feeling wary because we know of unscrupulous individuals who have sought to manipulate others for their personal financial benefit. Such opportunists are no more than cheap charlatans, and the harm they do to the cause of Christ is reprehensible. But their existence doesn't mean we should overlook what God has explicitly encouraged and commanded us to do. We must seek out godly leaders and Bible-believing churches and make sure the support we give to them is truly used to advance the kingdom of God.

Remember this positive truth from Scripture: "Make up your own mind what you will give. That will protect you against sob stories and arm-twisting. God loves it when the giver delights in the giving" (2 Corinthians 9:7, MSG).

It's been said that we can give to Christ without loving, but it is impossible to love Him without giving. The miracle is that, when we give from our hearts, the *more* we give the more goodness we receive. As Proverbs puts it, "There is one who scatters, yet increases more; and there is one who withholds more than is right, but it leads to poverty" (11:24). *The Message* translates this wisdom: "The world of the generous gets larger and larger; the world of the stingy gets smaller and smaller."

Enlarge your world; give of yourself and your possessions. God's investment principles work, and His dividends are unsurpassed!

35

Enlightening the Long, Dark Hours

THE FIRST COUNSEL I EVER RECEIVED concerning the nagging problem of insomnia came from a doctor at a famous California medical center. Abruptly brushing off my dilemma with a shrug, the physician bluntly suggested, "Oh, I've got that problem too. But there's no use losing any sleep over it!"

With a twinkle in his eye, he added one more tidbit of pseudo-comfort. He observed that, despite personal aggravations and annoyances, in all the annals of medical history no one has ever officially died from insomnia. (That's precious little comfort on a night when you feel trapped and tormented, unable to go to sleep!)

More than twenty-five million Americans wrestle (sometimes literally) with the problem of insomnia, tossing and turning throughout those dark, lonely hours when sleep refuses to come. What we want seems like such a little thing—and such an impossible dream: simply to get a decent night's rest.

If you have ever had trouble falling asleep, you know the misery insomnia can cause. Unfortunately, recent studies show that growing older can intensify that difficulty. As we age, we often have more trouble falling asleep and staying asleep. Many of us frequently awaken during the night and then lie there for hours, listening to our spouse breathe…or the windows rattle…or the refrigerator hum…or the faucet drip…or the house creak…

It's vitally important at this point to note that I'm talking about insomnia—difficulty falling asleep or waking up too early and not being able to go back to sleep. I'm not referring to the more serious problems that definitely need corrective medical attention to prevent serious complications.

Though it's nothing to brag about, I do claim some expertise when it comes to discussing insomnia. Over the past two decades I've struggled mightily with the problem (and let me assure you, it can be quite exhausting to work hard at falling asleep!). I have tried sophisticated sleep centers, biofeedback, hypnosis, and extensive neurological testing. I have consulted medical doctors, sleep specialists, psychiatrists, and psychological counselors. I have experimented with both naturopathic and homeopathic regimens as well as prescription medications and a panoply of well-intentioned home remedies, health foods, and "old wives'" panaceas. And yes, I have searched my own heart to see what message the Lord may be trying to present to me. Recently a friend mischievously suggested one cure for insomnia that I'd love to try: a good night's sleep!

Everything but that one I have tried. But, for me, there have been no obvious, lasting solutions, no sustained relief.

Still, I have learned a few lessons I gladly share (while cautioning that I'm not a medical doctor or a psychiatrist—just an experienced lay practitioner of insomnia!). I profoundly wish that early on I had avoided prescription drugs as even a temporary solution; I know now that they are *not* a good idea for alleviating long-term struggles.

I've also learned that one of the best remedies is simply resting quietly, waiting patiently for sleep to come and realizing, as the doctor said, that no one has ever died of insomnia. To fill the time as I wait, I sometimes list those friends for whom I have promised to pray. At other times I go through the alphabet, using each letter to define one of the characteristics of God, remember Bible verses, pray for friends and family members by name, or recall hymns and choruses.

One verse my mind used to hang on was Psalm 127:2. The King James Version translates it, "For so he giveth his beloved sleep." Since I *know* my love for the Lord is reciprocal, I couldn't understand why he didn't give *me* sleep. Then I discovered a different translation and was greatly encouraged. Its rendering teaches: "For He gives to His beloved even in his sleep" (NASB).

Now I recite this verse in the long hours before dawn and see God's hand of blessing *always* outstretched toward us day or night. Whether we are awake or asleep, His gracious mercies are constantly showered upon His children. Then I remember the twenty-first chapter of Revelation, which assures us of all the earthly miseries that exist "no more" in heaven; for me (and perhaps for my fellow insomniacs as well) the best realization is that there will be no more *night!*

36

After Retirement

IF EVER THERE IS A SEASON when a couple's marriage relationship is severely tested, it's retirement. Statistics reveal that after the
children are gone, the careers are set aside, and the schedules have
been radically altered, difficult adjustments are necessary to maintain harmony in a marriage. If a couple can't or won't made these
adjustments, it isn't unusual to find them enmeshed in painful
divorce proceedings, regardless of how long they've been married.

The "trick" to making these retirement adjustments is to find
ways to rekindle those original sparks that fanned into romantic
flames of love so long ago. In Revelation 2:4, Jesus told the church
of Ephesus, "You have left your first love." In other words, the
church that had begun with such zealous adoration for the Savior
had drifted away from that enthusiastic love. In the same way,
husbands and wives can easily drift away from their "first love"
and find themselves merely living together, tolerating each other's
differences with growing irritation and wondering what happened.

As we discussed earlier, the problem might be one of im-
maturity, despite the spouses' advanced age. Perhaps they have
the attitude of the little boy who wrote this essay on love:

> Love is something that makes two people think they
> are pretty when nobody else does. It also makes them

sit close together on a bench, when there is plenty of room on both ends.

Love is something that young people have, but that old people *don't* have, because it is all about dimples, and star-like eyes, and curls that old folks don't have. It is something that makes two people very quiet when you are around; also very quiet when you aren't, only in a different way. When they talk, it's all about dreams and roses and moonbeams.

When I grow up, I'm *not* going to fall in love. But if I do, she's got to let me say what to do and let me run everything. And that's what I know about love until I grow up.

Some of us *still* need to learn the same lesson this little boy is yet to discover. I think we men, in particular, have some things to learn as we enter retirement. *The Message* paraphrases the Bible's instructions to us this way: "Be good husbands to your wives. Honor them, delight in them. As women they lack some of your advantages. But in the new life of God's grace, you're equals. Treat your wives, then, as equals so your prayers don't run aground" (1 Peter 3:7). "Go all out in your love for your wives, exactly as Christ did for the church—a love marked by giving, not getting" (Ephesians 5:25).

We treat our wives as equals when we stand ready to share household duties rather than expect our wives to maintain their full routine of chores while waiting hand and foot on their newly "liberated" spouses. Since so many of us are older than our wives, that stage may, by necessity, come later—we don't want to rush things! That reminds me of the husband who asked his wife of many years, "Honey, will you love me when I'm old and feeble?"

To which she wisely responded, "Well, of course I do!"

37

Increasing Our GNP
(Good News Productivity)

THE WORLD TENDS TO EXPECT us to become less and less productive as we grow older. But this is definitely not the way God looks at the aging process! He expects us to continue working on His behalf, maintaining our strength to spread His Word, serving as His ambassadors on Earth as long as we're able. As He told the children of Israel, "Take heed to yourself, and diligently keep yourself, lest you forget the things your eyes have seen, and lest they depart from your heart all the days of your life. And teach them to your children and grandchildren" (Deuteronomy 4:9).

Even though in retirement we may no longer be earning a paycheck, we have the opportunity to work for a far greater reward. We may no longer be producing worldly goods, but we have a tremendous "good" to offer others—the good news! As Peter said to the lame man at the gate of the temple, "Silver and gold I do not have, but what I do have I give you: In the name of Jesus Christ of Nazareth, rise up and walk" (Acts 3:6).

In our middle years and later, many of us, especially those living on fixed incomes, don't have "silver and gold" to give, but we have the name of Jesus to share—and plenty of time and opportunities to do so. As we model Christ's love and tell the story of salvation, we can help others "rise up and walk" their way to heaven!

So how do we increase our good news productivity? Here are some ideas for how we can enrich our spiritual fruitfulness:

First, we can spend more time reading and meditating on the Scriptures each day, deepening our roots in the soil of God's Word. I like to try different translations as I study, because I gain new insights from seeing how the various words and phrases are translated differently. There are also many excellent study guides, study Bibles, and daily devotional books that can enhance your walk through the Word. Some of them are classics written by saints of the past; others are modern editions penned by today's popular authors. Most of the daily readings begin or end with Scripture; after I've read the devotion, I like to examine the suggested Bible passages and study their contexts for further illumination and inspiration.

Second, we can make certain we keep "short accounts" with God. When we find ourselves falling, we must ask for the Lord's forgiveness immediately. All of our secret sins must be confessed to the Savior. We must not hang on to that which drove the nails through His hands and feet! It's also important to eliminate any unnecessary "weeds" in our lives, those activities (which may include mindlessly sitting in front of the television) that may not be sinful but are not beneficial in ultimately drawing us closer to the Lord. Look at your schedule and see how you spend your time.

Third, we need to remember that even older, well-trained grapevines have to be tended regularly. Jesus said, "Every branch that bears fruit He prunes, that it may bear more fruit" (John 15:2). We should be willing to cooperate with God's pruning process in our lives. How? Simply by asking Him to reveal and then to remove those things in us that aren't of lasting eternal value. When the extraneous distractions are eliminated, our strength can be channeled into more important and productive areas of service.

Finally, we must spend quality time waiting on the Lord. In the Garden of Gethsemane, Jesus told His disciples to "Watch and pray, lest you enter into temptation. The spirit indeed is willing, but the flesh is weak" (Matthew 26:41). He asks the same of us. To be ready for the harvest, we must continue our prayers, rejoicing always and praying "without ceasing," as Paul instructed us. We're to continue praying even when God's answers seem slow in coming. Maybe you've been praying for years for certain requests—perhaps the salvation or welfare of some of your children or grandchildren. Perhaps you have been interceding for a neighbor or friend. Don't give up! The Lord's timing is *never* less than perfect. Our responsibility is to *wait.* To be patient. When it comes to spiritual fruit-bearing, our greatest productivity doesn't necessarily happen overnight!

Now, here are some practical questions we can ask ourselves to assess our spiritual productivity:

- Am I more thirsty for God and His Word now than I was a year ago?
- Do I show love and patience toward those around me?
- Am I truly concerned about the spiritual (and physical) needs of others?

- By my faithful attendance and involvement, do I
  show concern for the church and God's kingdom?
- Am I totally aware of the power of temptation and
  the danger of yielding to sin in my life?
- Do I judge others for their actions while overlooking
  my own foibles?
- Has it become easier to forgive others, especially
  those who have hurt me deeply?
- Am I often thinking of heaven and of that day when
  I will see my Savior face to face?

When we leave the work force, the world may consider us retired, but God considers us lifetime workers in His garden. He expects us to cultivate and saturate ourselves in His Word, to anticipate what He is waiting and wanting to do in us and through us. And then we're to go out and sow the seed! Are you about to retire or retired already? Good! God's got work for you to do!

38

Get Out!

RECENTLY A CALIFORNIA WOMAN found herself constantly feeling discouraged and depressed. Deciding a ride somewhere would improve her spirits, she called the local cab company and asked to be taken to the beach. She loves the ocean. The experience was so enjoyable and exhilarating, she decided to go for a longer drive. So she called the same cabby who had taken her to the beach and arranged for him to take her on a nine-day trip all along the West Coast to British Columbia and back! Such a unique adventure made all of the newspapers.

The 3,128-mile odyssey cost the sixty-eight-year-old retired hotel worker forty-one hundred dollars in cab fare plus a 15 percent tip, in addition to food and lodging. (She and the cabby had separate rooms.) The woman explained to the *Los Angeles Times* reporter, "I just got despondent over nothing to do. Cabin fever set in and I decided things had to be changed. I needed a new outlook! It snapped me out of my blue funk." Her driver loved the idea and offered, "My bosses don't care how far I go, just so long as they get paid."

The woman told the reporter, "I'm now thinking of Banff. I've always wanted to go there." Replied the cabby, "I've got a full tank of gas and am ready to go whenever she says!"

Discouragement and despondency can be common problems for older people. Sometimes doing something entirely out of the ordinary is what it takes to get a new lease on life. I'm not refer-ring to clinical depression, a condition that requires professional help. But there are those times when we all experience feelings of being blue or down in the dumps. Statistics show that women become melancholy, or depressed, two to three times more often than men.

The remedy for these temporary bouts of discouragement and dejection isn't Valium, Prozac, or St. John's wort. It can be as simple as doing something out of the ordinary, like the California woman did. When we feel blue, we need to get out and do some-thing, enjoy some fresh air and scenery, either in our own back-yards—or across the continent.

Some jokester once said, "You know you're getting older if you find you get the same sensation from a rocking chair as you once did from a roller coaster!" Whenever we feel that kind of "leveling" occurring in our psyches, we know it's time to stir things up, do something different, have an adventure!

Another practical but significant factor in warding off feelings of despair revolves around two familiar words: proper nutrition. Consider the biblical account of what happened to Elijah after he enjoyed a victory over the wicked prophets of Baal. Exhaustion and depression eventually overtook him, and he ended up sit-ting under a broom tree, praying that he might die. Exhausted, he fell asleep, and an angel awakened him twice and fed him. "Arise and eat, because the journey is too great for you," the angel said (see 1 Kings 19:1-8).

Even a single deficiency in our diets can trigger feelings of gloom, despair, and hopelessness. The possibility of nutrition playing a role in depression is especially true in someone who has recently lost a lifelong spouse. If this is your situation, you may not feel like eating, and the resulting lack of proper nutrition can make your depression even worse. It's a good idea to have someone keep an eye on your food intake and living conditions when you face a challenge that seems temporarily beyond your capabilities.

A third way we can chase away those dark clouds of doubt—and surely it's the easiest way—is simply to recount all that the Lord has done for us. Billy Bray, the famous Welsh coal-miner revivalist of another era, used to testify, "Yes, the Lord's given me both honey and vinegar. But I praise Him that He has given me vinegar with a teaspoon and honey with a ladle!"

Too often we are like the children of Israel who constantly grumbled as they trudged, becoming blind to all the miracles God was providing for them as they made their way through the wilderness. Similarly, we, too, may fail to see all the abundance, blessings, and mercies He showers constantly upon us. That's why it's important to get out and get into God's creation, seeing anew what a wonder it is.

A favorite story has a frustrated rabbi trying to motivate his disheartened congregation. "Don't you remember how our forefathers crossed the Red Sea dry-shod?" he asked. "Don't you remember how, for years without fail, they were fed with manna from heaven? Don't you remember how, when entering the Promised Land, our enemies fell on their faces, defeated before us?"

Only one woeful response came back. "Yes, we remember," a whiny voice replied. "But what has He done for us lately?"

We all need to get outside and consider what God has done for us *today* and every day. Doing so can be an uplifting and inspiring experience that lifts us from the gloom of self-pity. It worked for the psalmist! He wrote, "When I consider Your heavens, the work of Your fingers, the moon and the stars, which You have ordained, what is man that You are mindful of him?" (Psalm 8:3-4). Another passage says, "I'm thanking you, GOD, from a full heart, I'm writing the book on your wonders. I'm whistling, laughing, and jumping for joy; I'm singing your song, High God" (Psalm 9:1-2, MSG). Such images remind us of a scriptural corollary, found in the book of Proverbs: "A merry heart does good, like medicine" (Proverbs 17:22). Another translation puts it, "A cheerful disposition is good for your health; gloom and doom leave you bone-tired" (MSG).

There is one other dimension to consider, and it should really come first in the list of depression fighters, at least for believers in Jesus Christ. We need to ask the Lord to search our hearts, find the cause for our gloom or disappointment, and then help us get our priorities straight. This is what the psalmist did when he prayed, "Why are you down in the dumps, dear soul? Why are you crying the blues? Fix my eyes on God—soon I'll be praising again. He puts a smile on my face" (Psalm 42:5, MSG).

When you're stuck in the blues, fix your eyes on God and His wonderful creation. Get out, get going, and get happy!

39

Striving for Integrity

CONSISTENT, GENUINE INTEGRITY is one of our most valuable
assets as Christians.

The dictionary defines integrity as being "complete and in an
unbroken condition; whole; unimpaired, with sound moral principles." As Christians, we're to demonstrate integrity in even the
smallest issues of life. This includes paying bills on time, keeping our word even when it costs us personally, and treating others
kindly and fairly, especially those who previously have caused us
grief and trouble. We're to treat everybody equally lest we become
double-standard people, the kind of individuals James described
as "unstable in all [their] ways" (James 1:8). He spelled out a lesson for Christians in learning to treat everyone equally in the
second chapter of his letter:

> If a man enters your church wearing an expensive
> suit, and a street person wearing rags comes in
> right after him, and you say to the man in the suit,
> "Sit here, sir; this is the best seat in the house!" and
> either ignore the street person or say, "Better sit
> here in the back row," haven't you segregated God's
> children and proved that you are judges who can't
> be trusted?

...Isn't it clear by now that God operates quite differently? (2:2-5, MSG)

As people of integrity, we must extend the same love of Christ to the rich and the poor, the kind and the irritating. We must be scrupulously honest, trustworthy, and straightforward in maintaining solid biblical principles.

Too often we notice a lack of integrity among our elected officials, especially those who have held office awhile and gained considerable power. Why is it that young politicians enter office with such high and noble ambitions, promising to be totally honest and completely accountable and then, after a few years of hidden governmental "perks," we suspect that their well-intentioned integrity has become simple greed?

As someone said, "Integrity's a lot like oxygen: The higher you go, the more you need of it!" Unfortunately, we've seen the integrity of some of our highest elected leaders seeming to dissolve in recent times. This lack of integrity is one of the first signs of moral deterioration.

Integrity involves both character and reputation. Reputation is what *others think* us to be. Character is what *God knows* us to be. The book of Hebrews tells us everything is "open and laid bare" (4:13, NASB) before Almighty God, to whom we are ultimately accountable and responsible for our actions.

It is a tragic mistake to think there are somehow *degrees* of integrity. That just isn't so—not in the Lord's sight. When it comes to the moral issues of our day, wrong is always wrong, even if *everybody* does it. And conversely, right is right, even if *nobody* does it!

The great danger facing Christians is that we become too adept at rationalizing our actions. The truth is, the human conscience cannot be trusted as a reliable barometer for self-justification. Paul warned us that some people's consciences have been distorted with lies that have been burned into them as though "seared with a hot iron" (1 Timothy 4:2). When we allow ourselves to be controlled by such corrupted morals, it is very easy to justify ungodly actions. Eventually we get to the point that we believe we are right even when we're committing what Scripture openly calls transgressions. Nowhere is this more true than when it comes to sexual sins.

The Bible *never* excuses wickedness with a blanket absolution, such as the foolish excuse that "the Lord wants me to be happy."

The older we get, the more we should exhibit the hallmark of integrity. Others should see it from every aspect of our consistent living and our modeling of the characteristics of truth, honesty, and genuineness. It is unquestionably the standard I strive for as I approach the upward call, saying with Paul, "Not that I have already attained, or am already perfected; but I press on, that I may lay hold of that for which Christ Jesus has also laid hold of me" (Philippians 3:12).

It's not always easy to do what's right, even when we know that after all the chapters of life's book have been written, it is not how much money we have made, how many important positions we have held, or how many executive committees we have served on that will be important. Rather, it's our personal integrity that will matter most as we stand before Christ's judgment seat.

Then we will echo the testimony of Job, who, though severely tried and tested, earnestly prayed, "Let me be weighed in a just balance, that God may know my integrity" (Job 31:6).

40

Remembering What to Forget

"I KNOW I'M GETTING OLDER," someone told me recently, "because I keep making mental notes to myself and then forgetting where I put them!"

Another person solved the mental-note problem by writing things down. "Now I write down everything I want to remember," he said. "That way, instead of spending a lot of time trying to remember what I wrote down, I spend the time looking for the paper where I wrote it!"

As we age, we tend to forget things and lose our belongings. As one senior citizen quipped, "Happiness is finding your glasses before you forget *why* you wanted them in the first place." It seems in our later years we more frequently forget names. Then we forget faces. And next we forget...

Sorry! I forgot where I was going with this thought...

Oh yes, forgetfulness!

Do you find yourself having more trouble remembering things as each year passes, often confusing names and details? Well, don't think you're suffering a problem that afflicts only the aged! I don't know the source of the following list, but it supposedly came from a sixth-grade Sunday school class that was surveyed to see how much the youngsters knew about the Bible. Read the answers the students gave, and you may not feel so bad about *your* memory!

- "The first book of the Bible is Guinesses, in which Adam and Eve were created from an apple tree."
- "Noah's wife was called Joan of Ark."
- "Samson slayed the Philistines with the ax of the apostles."
- "Unleavened bread is bread made without ingredients."
- "Moses went to the top of My Cyanide to get the 10 Commandments."
- "Joshua led the Hebrews in the battle of Geritol."
- "David fought with the Finkelsteins, a race of people who lived in biblical times."
- "The people who follow Jesus were called the twelve decibels."
- "One of the opossums was Saint Matthew."

While it's usually a nuisance, if not an embarrassment, to forget a date or name or fact we really want to remember, forgetting some things isn't bad at all. For example, Paul himself forcefully declared, "One thing I do, forgetting those things which are behind and reaching forward to those things which are ahead, I press toward the goal for the prize of the upward call of God in Christ Jesus" (Philippians 3:13-14).

Paul was reminding us there are things we *should* forget. Unfortunately, those are the things that sometimes seem to stick most tenaciously in our memories! For instance, do you have trouble forgetting an unkind word a person may have said to you? Probably not! Or how about a promise someone has failed to keep? Do you have to work to remember a complaint some-one made about your work or your actions?

In marriage it is especially helpful if both husband and wife can forget a few things: hurts for which an apology has been offered and accepted; insignificant irritants that, unless they are forgiven and forgotten, have the potential to make spouses im-patient and angry; all the little annoyances that will make absolutely *no* difference when we are called to glory! Actually, once we start thinking about all the inconsequential matters that tend to stick in our minds and make us miserable, we come to agree with Jack Hayford, who says, "We can hardly overestimate the relative unimportance of almost everything!"

Some of us allow remembered *negatives* to become the rul-ing passion of our lives while, ironically, those who have slighted us have totally forgotten why we are angry at them! Such a situa-tion proves the point that we don't hold grudges—they hold *us,* like an ever-tightening and restrictive vice. Think about this: If God casts *our* sins into the "depths of the sea" (Micah 7:19), He can help us cast our grudges into the vast sea of our forget-fulness. Ask Him to help you heave those heavy burdens right into the ocean. On their way down, they may just knock loose a happy thought you wanted to remember! As it bubbles to the surface, *don't forget* to say, "Thank You, Lord!"

41

Heartily Useful

IN THE SIGHT OF GOD, there is never a time in our lives when we lose our potential to be useful. Remember that fact as you prepare to retire—or as you plan the next stage of your retirement. Too many folks seem to spend their later years taking "Scottish vacations." (That is when you stay at home but let your mind wander!)

When you decide to retire, don't sit around waiting for the telephone to ring. Instead, proactively volunteer; determine that you will use your God-given talents in whatever way He may desire. There really is no limit to what older people can accomplish if we are willing to try. For example,

- Michelangelo, at age eighty-eight, was still painting churches.
- Peter Roget updated his *Thesaurus* not long before he died at ninety.
- Alexander Graham Bell kept inventing right up to his death.
- Benjamin Franklin helped write the U.S. Constitution when he was eighty-one.
- Claude Monet painted until age eighty-five!

All of these people obviously chose to be useful right up to the very end! Or maybe they just never stopped to think about whether they were too old to be doing what they were doing. They were too busy doing it!

We have all been gifted with unique talents, and we should never stop contributing our gifts as long as we are able. The best way to get over any feelings of uselessness is to go out and do something positive and worthwhile for someone else. Certainly we shouldn't hesitate to try something new just because some eyebrows might rise to see someone our age attempting it. As opera star Beverly Sills encouragingly said, "You may be disappointed if you fail, but you'll be *doomed* if you don't try."

My friend Stuart Briscoe tells about his godly mother, who was saved late in life. She felt that, as "only" a housewife, there was little she could accomplish for the Lord. So she made certain her home was always in order, ready at any moment for the Savior's return. And over her kitchen sink she placed a little sign that read, "Divine services are held here three times daily."

Some of us, due to physical limitations, don't have the option of painting churches or serving in government or volunteering in soup kitchens. Maybe all we can do is stand at the sink (or kneel by our beds) and pray. The point is to do "heartily, as for the Lord" whatever we can do wherever we are (Colossians 3:23, NASB). Like the old extrabiblical beatitude avows, "Blessed is the man who willingly serves as a member of the committee he wanted to chair." We can't always have the most prestigious, attention-getting positions. Sometimes we have to play second fiddle, be the dishwasher instead of the chef, sell the popcorn in the stands instead of hitting the winning home run. The important thing is that we get out there and do it! Then, as the psalmist proclaimed, "Those who are planted in the house of the LORD shall flourish in the courts of our God. They shall still bear fruit in old age" (Psalm 92:13-14).

42

Love Note

A LITTLE GIRL WAS PLACED in an orphanage because her mother felt she could no longer keep her. The child was quite unattractive and had many annoying mannerisms. As a result, she was always shunned by the other children and fervently disliked by her teachers.

The head of the orphanage was constantly searching for a reason to send her off to a reform school or a youth detention center. One afternoon the opportunity finally came. The little girl was suspected of writing clandestine notes to people outside the orphanage, a practice that was strictly forbidden in the institution. One of the other children reported to the superintendent, "I saw her write a message and hide it on a tree by the stone wall."

Smugly, the superintendent hurried to the tree that jutted out over the wall. She found the note stuck to a twig on a limb overhanging the sidewalk. Hurriedly she unfolded it, read the childish marks, then passed it silently to her assistant.

With tears quickly filling her eyes, the secretary silently read, "To whoever finds this: I love you!"

Without question, the best gift God gives to children is someone who loves them—usually dedicated moms and dads. When those parents teach their children to love and serve their Creator, they enjoy the ultimate legacy of life: seeing their children grow up to know the Savior, loving God's Word, and seeking constantly to follow His will.

This isn't to overlook those children—perhaps you were one of them—who were not fortunate enough to have been reared in a Christian home. You may reflect on difficulties within the home where you grew up and find no happy memories whatsoever. You may even have suffered through the same predicament King David described, saying, "My father and mother walked out and left me" (Psalm 27:10, MSG). We don't know the specific details David was alluding to, but we do know "the rest of the story," as Paul Harvey would say. We know, because David declared in the very next line, "But GOD took me in."

Like David, Christians can draw comfort in knowing that no matter what happened to us as children, God has taken us in. Even today, our heavenly Father knows all our circumstances as well as all our needs.

Scripture further assures us that we are all special to the Lord. Most children are considered special by their earthly parents too. But there are human exceptions. Our world has witnessed the tragedy of parents who neglect their children, sometimes to the point that the little ones suffer and even die. There are mothers who, because of their own addictions and obsessive behaviors, turn away from their offspring, sometimes completely abandoning them. What a comfort to know this will *never* happen to us as children of God. He loves us so much He has engraved our names on the palms of His hands; they are always before Him (see Isaiah 49:16)! And God promises us that He has "plans for

[your] welfare and not for calamity to give you a future and a hope" (Jeremiah 29:11, NASB).

That hope comes in a powerful message someone left for us on a tree outside a city wall. Like the little girl in the orphanage, that Person was "despised and rejected" (Isaiah 53:3). In a place called Calvary, the people tried to get rid of this "intruder." But His message has reverberated through the centuries and speaks to us even today. Anyone who goes to the cross where Jesus died will find the Word of the ultimate Parent hanging from a nail. It's a message that reads, "To whoever finds this: I love you!"

43

The Latest Fad at the Cemetery

HAVE YOU HEARD ABOUT the newest trend in "designer" grave-stones? The *Los Angeles Times* recently carried a fascinating article describing how customized granite markers are being made in the form of whatever the person's interest was during life. For example, some monuments have been carved in the shape of ten-nis rackets, bowling balls, sewing machines, golf clubs, juke-boxes—even a B-1 bomber! One man had a granite parking meter installed atop his tomb. The coin slots were welded shut, and appropriately the red flag had come up reading, "Expired."

The Southern California gravestone of Mel Blanc is reported to have a unique epithet. Blanc was the famed voice of Jack Benny's antiquated Maxwell automobile as well as a number of cartoon characters, including the famous Porky Pig. His marker bears Porky's familiar signoff, "Th-th-th-that's all folks!"

As I read about these fancy tombstones, a modern translation of Psalm 49:10-12 came to mind: "Anyone can see that the bright-est and best die, wiped out right along with fools and dunces. They leave all their prowess behind, move into their new home, The Coffin, the cemetery their permanent address.... We aren't immor-tal. We don't last long.... We age and weaken. And die" (MSG).

A coffin beneath the most elaborate grave marker is still just a coffin! And there's only one way we can keep from making that box our permanent home: Jesus! He has assured us of our unmistakable future, promising, "I go and prepare a place for you" (John 14:3). *That's* the home I'm dying to move in to!

It's okay to have a tombstone shaped like a bowling ball. There's no crime (at least in most places) in asking that our graves be decorated with the likeness of a parking meter or a jukebox, if that brings comfort to our families. But don't think for a minute it will bring any comfort to *us* when our funeral services end and the mourners go home. As believers, we'll already be parked at the heavenly throne, gazing into the loving eyes of God and listening to the music of the angels! We won't give a second thought to the silly baubles we've left behind—whether they be luxurious mansions or designer tombstones.

For the Christian there need be no fear of death. Nothing expresses that better to me than this old prose, whose author is unknown:

> I am standing on the seashore. A ship at my side
> spreads her white sails to the morning breeze and
> starts for the blue ocean. She is an object of beauty
> and strength, and I stand watching her until at
> length she is only a speck of white cloud just where
> the sea and sky meet and mingle with each other.
> Then someone at my side exclaims, "There, she's
> gone."
>
> Gone where? Gone from my sight, that is all. She is
> just as large in hull and mast and spar as she was
> when she left my side, and just as able to bear her

load of living freight to the place of her destination.
Her diminished size is in me, not in her.

And just at the moment when someone at my side
says, "She's gone," there are others watching for her
coming and other voices ready to take up the glad
shout, "There, she comes."

And that is dying.

We have Jesus' absolute promise that He will take us to be with
Him forever. Rather than a coffin, our new home will be that
place described so beautifully in the words of the old gospel song,

There's a land that is fairer than day,
And by faith we can see it afar;
For the Father waits over the way
To prepare us a dwelling place there.

Now, let the chorus wash over your mind and heart:

In the sweet by and by,
We shall meet on that beautiful shore.
In the sweet by and by,
We shall meet on that beautiful shore!

And here's another inspiring description of our heavenly home,
developed by my friend Don Wyrtzen. He took an old "gem"
and polished it into new musical luster with his song "Finally
Home."

When engulfed by the terror of tempestuous seas,
Unknown waves before you roll.
At the end of doubt and peril is eternity,
Though fear and conflict seize your soul.
When surrounded by the blackness of the darkest
night,
Oh, how lonely death can be.
At the end of this long tunnel there is Christ, the
shining Light,
For death is swallowed up in victory.
But just think of stepping on shore and finding it
heaven,
Of touching a hand, and finding it God's,
Of breathing new air, and finding it celestial,
Of waking up in glory, and finding it Home.[1]

All I can add is...*Amen!*

1. Reprinted by permission of Don Wyrtzen.

44

Ready for Immediate Departure!

PREPARING TO LEAVE on a recent flight, the attendants were bustling about the cabin, helping passengers find their seats, stow their luggage, and buckle their seat belts. Then came an announcement over the PA system: "If everyone will please be seated, we are ready for *immediate* departure!"

Hearing that command, I had to smile. Those four words summarize perfectly how I desire to live my life: ready for *immediate* departure. Should the Lord call me to glory this year, this month, *this minute,* I want to be ready to go! That's one reason why one of my favorite Scripture verses is the affirmation I seek each day to emulate: "Looking for the blessed hope and glorious appearing of our great God and Savior Jesus Christ" (Titus 2:13).

Being ready for heaven doesn't mean that our focus should be *only* on the hereafter. We don't want to be the kind of people Vance Havner used to describe as "so *heavenly* minded they're no *earthly* good." We need to keep heaven in our hearts while being mindful of how we spend our limited time here on earth. These hours and minutes and seconds will never be given to us again, so we need to make sure we invest them wisely.

I tease our daughter-in-law that she is the world's greatest "returner." I call her "the poster girl for Nordstrom's 'returns department.'" No matter what she's bought, if she finds a flaw or if it turns out that the item doesn't quite meet her needs, she has no shame in taking it back for an exchange or a full refund. But there's no returning the time we're given here on earth. This is it; this is all the time we're given to spend—and only once!

If we spend all our limited time accumulating earthly treasures, we may find ourselves in a predicament like the one theologian Ray Stedman used to describe. Stedman, who is now home with the Lord, worked his way through seminary as a part-time mortuary employee. In need of a dark blue suit for preaching assignments, he noticed how the undertaker could purchase garments for the deceased at incredibly low, wholesale prices. Being an impoverished student and realizing what a savings he could make, Stedman asked if he might have the opportunity to purchase a suit from the undertaker's supplier.

When the mortician agreed, Stedman quickly placed his order. He could hardly wait for the new garment to arrive, looking forward to having something dignified to wear in his increasing pulpit duties. You can imagine his surprise, however, on that first Sunday morning when he pulled on the suit. He started to put his wallet into the back pocket and his keys into the front pocket. Only then did he discover that the new suit had absolutely *no* pockets.

When you stop to think about it, that only makes good sense. In clothing a dead man, pockets would be a superfluous expense. As the psalmist wrote, "When he dies he shall carry nothing away" (Psalm 49:17). Or as the comedian quipped, you never see a hearse pulling a U-Haul!

Perhaps that verse from Psalm 49 was what writer Max Lucado had in mind when he suggested that we make our major life decisions while visiting a cemetery. Like the burial clothes with no pockets, that setting would certainly help us put our decision-making into perspective, wouldn't it! Being able to reason with this kind of depth and discernment is what distinguishes mere *knowledge* from *wisdom*. As one person put it, "Wisdom is what you gain after you think you know it all." A person who's only educated in "book learning" but not wise toward God is actually nothing more than an educated fool.

We're told repeatedly in Psalms and Proverbs that wisdom begins with "the fear of the Lord." (Recently I have been greatly blessed on this subject by reading some chapters from Jerry Bridges's excellent book titled *The Joy of Fearing God*.) As one who understands this "fear," imagine yourself standing in that cemetery at the beginning of your last day on earth, deciding how you will spend your remaining hours and minutes. Would you be planning your time with more careful thought and deliberation than you normally do? Would you be ready for immediate departure?

45

God's Best

ONE OF THE MOST EXCITING BOOKS I read as a child growing up in Santa Barbara wasn't the one you might expect. It wasn't about the exploits of Tom Sawyer and Huck Finn nor about the alluring adventures of the Hardy Boys. This riveting tome was an entirely different kind of volume.

It was a huge mail-order catalog that we kids often pored over, especially on rainy days or when we had to stay home from school because we were sick. Back then every item in the catalog was offered in three different columns: Good, Better, and Best (with three escalated prices affixed to each product). In those days of the Great Depression, we could only daydream about owning the merchandise from the Best column.

Today I think of that catalog when I realize how tragic it is that too many of us, even "dedicated" Christians, settle for only the *good* in life. Rather than seeking God's will and striving for the very *best*, we get distracted by choices that bring temporary satisfaction instead of eternal joy. This is why Scripture urges us to "earnestly desire the best gifts" (1 Corinthians 12:31).

It may be that you're at a stage in your life when you may feel "good" but ordinary—a believer but not of very much use to God or even to yourself. Such an attitude often develops from a mind-set of comfortable contentment as we sit on the sidelines.

We watch other people accomplishing great feats for the Lord and marvel at their talents and confidence, never imagining that we, too, have talents and gifts to share.

We need to get down out of the grandstands and take our positions on the playing field of life. We have all been blessed with "diversities of gifts, but the same Spirit...differences of ministries, but the same Lord...diversities of activities, but it is the same God who works all in all" (1 Corinthians 12:4-6). You may not feel qualified to speak before large audiences or to teach a Bible study or to take the Lord's Supper to shut-ins. Humanly speaking, none of us is! But God has given us "diversities of gifts," and it's our assignment to use those gifts in His service. Consider your God-given talents and unique abilities, and don't argue that you have none! They are there! All of us have been blessed with them. But each of us is a distinctive creation of the Lord! He still hasn't made any two of us alike, so your gifts may not be the same as anyone else's.

Remember, too, that as we allow Him, God will make changes in us so that we can do things we may not think we can accomplish at first. It's true that God loves us just the way we are; however, He also loves us too much to leave us *just* the way we are! His purpose is to accomplish what's best for us—that which is "exceeding abundantly above all that we ask or think" (Ephesians 3:20, KJV).

Some people live their Christianity so shallowly that they appear to be taking care not to offend the devil! To reach toward God's best means that we follow a path of increasing depth and enrichment in our relationship with Him. As we travel that path we enjoy progressive sanctification, for "He who has begun a good work in you will complete it until the day of Jesus Christ" (Philippians 1:6).

As a child, I used to dream about owning things from the Best column in the mail-order catalog. As an adult, I set similar goals in pursuing God's best for me, His perfect and appointed plan for my life. In the Great Depression, my childhood dreams for the best things in life seemed impossibly out of reach. But in God's holy kingdom, the Father works in us so that we may have "what is well pleasing in His sight, through Jesus Christ, to whom be glory forever and ever. Amen" (Hebrews 13:21).

46

Are You Suffering...or Pregnant with Joyful Anticipation?

A PAIN BOILS UP IN MY CHEST, and I wonder, *Is this a heart attack?* I notice a new mole on my shoulder and think, *It may be melanoma!* My arm "falls asleep," and I worry, *Stroke!* My stomach hurts, and I think, *Do I have gallstones or pancreatic cancer?*

As we grow older, we come into increasing contact with those who have endured (or succumbed to) these and other medical problems. Suddenly it seems that every edition of the newspaper reports some frightening new prediction or complication. For instance, current statistics indicate that more than 75 percent of older people *will* face at least one of the three most debilitating health problems: heart attack, stroke, or cancer. I saw an amazing warning somewhere that said when it comes to prostate cancer, if a man lives long enough, there's practically a 100 percent certainty this problem will eventually befall him.

We all wonder if one of these disasters is lurking somewhere in our future. Perhaps without even being conscious of it, we stand on alert, waiting for the "other shoe" to drop.

It's wise to be aware of early symptoms and to maintain a healthy lifestyle that helps protect us from these ailments as much as possible, but as Christians, our position isn't to *conquer* death (Christ has already done that). We welcome the seemingly

continual announcements that scientists are discovering new pre-
ventions, treatments, and even cures for these problems. But our
earnest desire is not to avoid death but simply to live life to the
fullest, right up to the very end, however that end may come!

My friend Joni Eareckson Tada hasn't hesitated to pray for
physical healing that would make her wheelchair and life support unnecessary. But healing hasn't been God's will for Joni. And
one wonders whether she would be so blessed today with such a
worldwide ministry if she weren't confined to that wheelchair.
Similarly, the apostle Paul prayed that his "thorn in the flesh"
(2 Corinthians 12:7) might be removed. It apparently wasn't, but
his Spirit-inspired words have long outlived his problem, comforting us now, nearly two thousand years later. Jesus also prayed,
even though He foreknew His divine mission, and God didn't
see fit to remove the cup of suffering from His hands.

The purpose of prayer is not to overcome God's reluctance but
to make certain our desires are in accordance with His will. That
is the only way to take hold firmly of His gracious providence.

So what is the best remedy for any physically or mentally
debilitating illnesses? In a word, it's *hope!* I love this definition
someone gave:

> Hope is not the conviction that something will turn
> out well but rather it is the certainty that something
> makes sense, regardless of how it all turns out.

To explain how this remedy "works," we often turn to Romans
8:24-25, the familiar passage that states, "For in hope we have

been saved, but hope that is seen is not hope; for why does one also hope for what he sees? But if we hope for what we do not see, with perseverance we wait eagerly for it" (NASB). *The Message,* however, casts these verses in a rather unexpected way. It may take a second (or even a third) reading to grasp this concept, presented here so differently. It says:

> The difficult times of pain throughout the world are simply birth pangs. But it's not only around us; it's *within* us. The Spirit of God is arousing us within. We're also feeling the birth pangs. These sterile and barren bodies of ours are yearning for full deliverance. That is why waiting does not diminish us, any more than waiting diminishes a pregnant mother. We are enlarged in the waiting. We, of course, don't see what is enlarging us. But the longer we wait, the larger we become, and the more joyful our expectancy.
>
> Meanwhile, the moment we get tired in the waiting, God's Spirit is right alongside helping us along.

Well, *that* certainly puts a new spin on things, doesn't it? Could you, if you find yourself debilitated by a heart attack, a stroke, a cancer, a wheelchair—*whatever,* imagine that you are not struck down by suffering but instead *pregnant* with a joyful attitude of expectancy? As a man, just considering such an image makes me smile (it may not have the same effect on you women!). But I believe that was Paul's point, that we should draw on God's strength and His promises of eternal happiness to keep us smiling through our earthly adversities.

If God sees fit to give you a thorn in your flesh, if He extends to you a cup of pain or sorrow, pray that He will also guide and direct you so that His name may be glorified through your suffering. And then let yourself be *enlarged* with anticipation of the joy to come.

47

Shake Things Up!

IT WAS VANCE HAVNER who sagely observed, "Too many services begin at eleven o'clock sharp and end at twelve noon dull!" He probably recited the same Sunday morning prayer as the old Scottish deacon who, before every service, would plead, "Oh, Lord, please let something happen today that's not already printed in the bulletin!"

The best preachers undoubtedly hope that something will happen in every worship service that will light a spark of fervor in the gathered Christians. They know that the most beautiful, expertly planned and presented worship services that occur week after week with exacting perfection can become mechanically monotonous. All too often, as Max Lucado observes, our worship services become more of a showplace instead of a place of worship. "It's almost as if we're trying to impress the Lord with how good *we* are, rather than simply confessing how *great* He is," Lucado said.

That was surely one of the reasons Charles Spurgeon prayed, "Please give your Church, Lord, a glorious season of 'divine' disorder." He was asking God to shake up the people as well as the program.

It is said that the first-century Christians used to infuriate and frustrate the secular society of their day, because no matter what

hardship they were enduring, they were *always* singing and praising the Lord. Believers of that era would even sing while paying their taxes. (I'm not sure how many people today would be
willing to follow such an incredible practice; nor would the
IRS know how to handle the situation if they did!)

It's easy for us older Christians to become set in our ways on
Sunday mornings, mindlessly following the order of service, recit-
ing the Lord's Prayer or perhaps a creed or two in a drone while
our minds wander elsewhere. We might even be tempted to doze
a bit through the sermon or keep an eye on our watches to see if
the preacher's staying on schedule. Does this kind of worship
really mean anything? And if it doesn't mean anything to us, then
how can we expect it to mean anything to God?

We need to be willing to try new approaches and new ideas
to give meaning and purpose to our times of worship and fellowship. Keep this fact in mind when your music director
announces one Sunday that the congregation will *sing* the Lord's
Prayer instead of *say* it. Remember it when the pastor inserts an
object lesson into the program, welcoming the little ones down
front for a moment or two. Think of it when the youth group
acts out a passage of Scripture in lieu of the regular sermon. If
we find a sarcastic comment or complaint forming in our minds
when such changes occur, we should realize instead that our
church leaders are trying to shake things up a bit—and keep us
awake!

In the third chapter of the book of James, the inspired writer
declared that, "the tongue is a little member" but can cause
untold damage and destruction (verse 5). Interestingly, the word

member in the original is "melody." God created this small but vocal part of our anatomy not for complaining but for the express purpose of praising Him.

Have you ever noticed how many different details appear along a familiar stretch of highway when construction or some other delay causes you to travel it at ten miles per hour instead of sixty? Maybe as you creep along you notice for the first time the wildflowers blooming along the shoulders or a hawk building its nest atop a utility pole. There may be an appealing little store tucked into a shopping center you usually whiz by without noticing or a cottage that reminds you of a favorite childhood story. All these things were there every day as you drove by, but something made you slow down and notice the richness of your surroundings.

The same can be true in worship. We can zip through the service without thinking...until something happens "that's not already printed in the bulletin." Then we slow down and take notice. Perhaps we feel ourselves being touched anew by the Lord's Prayer when its words are set to music. Maybe we reap a lesson of our own from the children's sermon.

Originally, the word *worship* meant "worth-ship," a term that referred to the price or value of an admired object. Do we show God how much we value Him by the way we worship Him? When we slide into the pew on Sunday morning, do we come ready to "worship the LORD in the splendor of his holiness" (1 Chronicles 16:29, NIV). Do we "tremble before Him" (verse 30)? As we sing His praises, do we sing in a way that would inspire anyone to proclaim, "Let the heavens rejoice, let the earth be glad;... Let the sea resound,...let the fields be jubilant" (16:31-32, NIV)? When we join other Christians in our churches, we should sense the presence of God in those places with us. We should feel assured that He's there, welcoming our praise and hearing our prayers.

During the years of their dedicated ministry, John and Charles Wesley experienced all kinds of rigorous privations, along with numerous trials and testings. They encountered situations and stress that would have made normal people give up. But the two dedicated brothers never wavered in their remarkable ministry. Historians tell us they praised God even with their dying breaths.

The memorial plaque in Westminster Abbey, which testifies to lifetimes of faithful service and consistent rejoicing, reads simply, "And, best of all, God was with us!"

When we gather to worship God, His presence among us is the best part of the service. Did you feel it? Or did you doze off?

48

Throw Open the Doors!

WHEN SORROW AND SUFFERING HIT, we are tempted to wonder, "Why me, Lord?" It might be more appropriate to ask instead, "What are You trying to teach me, Lord?"

The fact is, we seldom learn a great deal about God's will when things are going well. It is when the hard times and trials pound in upon us that we are forced, finally, to our *only* real resort—the Lord Himself!

For many of us, that lesson is one we have to relearn again and again. It's the one we must remember before God can teach us the *next* lessons He has planned for us. True, we may be able to survey the whole world while standing tall, but it's only when we're on our knees that we can "see" the Savior! It's when we're on our knees that life's most valuable lessons are learned. That's why prayer is such a tremendous force in molding our hearts and minds. In prayer we "throw open our doors to God and discover at the same moment that he has already thrown open his door to us" (Romans 5:2, MSG).

If you are going through trials and torment right now, throw open the doors of your heart and find God waiting for you there. Welcome Him into your life, for He is "our refuge and strength, an ever-present help in trouble" (Psalm 46:1, NIV). He will "never leave us nor forsake us" (1 Kings 8:57, NIV). He holds us in His right hand and says, "Fear not, I will help you" (Isaiah 41:13). He is our rock, our fortress, our deliverer, our strength, our shield, and our stronghold (see Psalm 18:2). In the midst of our misery, He gives us peace beyond anything we can understand (see Philippians 4:7). And though we weep through the night, He brings us joy in the morning (see Psalm 30:5).

Throw open the doors of your life to Him, and your life will never be the same. That's not to say your problems will instantly vanish and you'll never hurt again. But you'll find yourself strengthened and encouraged by His powerful love to face whatever must be faced.

Annie Johnson Flint has written one of my favorite verses on this subject. She calls it "One Day at a Time."

> One day at a time, with its failures and fears,
> With its hurts and mistakes, with its weakness and
>   tears,
> With its portion of pain and its burden of care;
> One day at a time we must meet and must bear.
>
> One day at a time to be patient and strong,
> To be calm under trial and sweet under wrong;
> Then its toiling shall pass and its sorrow shall cease;
> It shall darken and die, and the night shall bring peace.
>
> One day at a time—but the day is so long
> And the heart is not brave and the soul is not strong.
> O, Thou pitiful Christ, be Thou near all the way.
> Give courage and patience and strength for the day.

Swift cometh His answer, so clear and so sweet;
"Yea, I will be with thee, thy troubles to meet;
I will not forget thee, nor fail thee, nor grieve;
I will not forsake thee; I never will leave."

Not yesterday's load we are called on to bear,
Nor the morrow's uncertain and shadowy care;
Why should we look forward or back with dismay?
Our needs, as our mercies, are but for the day.

One day at a time, and the day is His day;
He hath numbered its hours, though they haste or
    delay.
His grace is sufficient; we walk not alone;
As the day, so the strength that He giveth His own.

49

Breaking the Cycle

FOR MANY OF US, getting older is a sobering reminder of the impact we are leaving on our families. Surely there is no greater legacy than a life others can easily and profitably emulate.

What kind of legacy are you leaving your family? What important decisions have you made that can be passed on to the next generation? Are they principles that really count for eternity? One would certainly hope such lessons would be a little more insightful than the one famed hotelier Conrad Hilton supposedly uttered. Asked by a reporter if he would like to leave a message for those who came after him, he responded, "Yes! Tell them the shower curtain goes *inside* the tub!"

Such mundane details aside, if we are involved in any harmful habits or sinful practices, *now* is the time to break that cycle before it can spiral downward through the next generations. We must give our children, grandchildren, and even our great-grandchildren the proper role model they can easily follow! Think about it: Would you want them to see what you are doing or thinking right now?

The Old Testament carefully describes the story of the Ten Commandments. It also gives straightforward, clear-cut warnings to those who fail to obey them. One of them is this sobering statement from the Almighty: "I, the LORD your God, am

154

a jealous God, visiting the iniquity of the fathers upon the children to the third and fourth generations of those who hate Me" (Deuteronomy 5:9).

Note what this verse *doesn't* say. It does not imply that we can excuse our failures with comments like, "Well, it's just in my genes. My great-grandfather was like that; I can't help the way I react!"

Regardless of our family tree, each of us is ultimately and personally responsible to God for everything we think and do! There is absolutely no excuse before the Lord. The writer of Hebrews puts it correctly, "Nothing...is hidden from God's sight. Everything is uncovered and laid bare before the eyes of him to whom we must give account" (4:13, NIV).

It's up to us, individually, to live according to God's commandments and example. We can't do anything about the legacy our forefathers have handed down to us, but we *can* have an impact on the legacy we hand down to those who come after us. If there's some "iniquity" in our lives that we don't want to see in our children and grandchildren, now is the time to confess that sin to God and claim another statement from the Almighty: "I will forgive their wickedness and will remember their sins no more" (Hebrews 8:12, NIV).

The Lord always extends His grace and kindness, even though there is necessary and required judgment. In His love He shows "mercy to thousands, to those who love Me and keep My commandments" (Deuteronomy 5:10).

50

One Day Closer to Heaven

ALL OF US, REGARDLESS OF AGE, have one thing in common. Obviously it's not material wealth, educational background, political affiliation, nor our employment records. Rather, it is the incontrovertible fact that we are *all* getting older!

Did I hear you groan? Perhaps you need an attitude adjustment!

Consider the famous story that occurred during World War II. Winston Churchill had done his best to buoy the spirits of his countrymen, but the fact was, England stood on the brink of not only disaster but also possible extinction. Then the United States declared war on Germany and joined the conflict. The venerable statesman was asked, "Do you think this is the beginning of the end?"

The cigar-chomping politician responded gruffly, "No, it's not. But it is the end of the beginning. Now we are assured of a glorious future conquest!"

We should think of retirement as a time of glorious future accomplishments, not as the beginning of the end. After all, the older we are, the closer we are to heaven, and the more we should sense God's presence every moment we live. His growing presence in our lives should be an exhilarating force in this life stage, motivating us to achieve new victories in His name.

Older people, having "been there, done that, heard it all," have
a tendency to forget this crucial *spiritual* dimension of life. Instead
of excitedly anticipating everything we've been taught about
heaven, our retirement years can take on an unfortunate sense of
dread and defeat. We tend to focus on the sadness of death rather
than on the tremendous happiness we'll enjoy one millisecond
after we die! If we find ourselves sinking into a defeated attitude,
we must remember that, as God has given us the necessary grace
to live this long, so, when it is time, He will likewise give us the
grace to face earth's final chapter. And then He will welcome us
into His everlasting arms!

Secular gerontologists can only advise us to accept death as the
inevitable conclusion to life. But as believers we know there's a
sequel—and it's even better than the original! It is the privilege
of believers to talk and think frankly about eternity and what
God has in store for us. Christians don't exist in "the land of
the living," while waiting to go to the "land of the dying." The
opposite is true. We're constantly reminded of two amazing con-
cepts: the shortness of time and the vastness of eternity!

It was Charles Wesley who in his later years wrote in his
journal:

> This day I enter my eighty-sixth year. I now find that
> I grow old. My sight is decaying so that I cannot read
> small print unless in a strong light. My strength is
> diminished, so that I walk much slower than I did
> some years ago. My memory of names, whether per-
> sons or places, is reduced. What I should be afraid of

is that, by the increase of bodily infirmities, my physical problems might weigh down my mind and create a stubbornness and unyielding attitude. But, Thou, O Lord my God, shalt continue to be my strength, and answer for me.

Remember, we are *all* growing older. Accepting that fact, stretch yourself! Risk a new challenge. Make a new acquaintance. Most of all, revel in the fact that we aren't at the *end* but rather at the glorious *beginning* of what God has in store for us.

About the Author

AFTER MORE THAN FIFTY-FIVE YEARS in professional broadcasting, Al Sanders is one of the best-known personalities in Christian radio today. He can be heard daily as the host for *Joni & Friends* with Joni Eareckson Tada and for *Telling the Truth* with Stuart and Jill Briscoe. Over the span of his career, Al has scripted, produced, or hosted many popular radio programs, including *BreakPoint* with Chuck Colson, *UpWords* with Max Lucado, *Insight for Living* with Chuck Swindoll, and Jack Hayford's *Living Way* broadcast ministry.

Currently, Al serves as chairman of the board for Ambassador Advertising Agency, which he founded in 1959. Today Ambassador provides support to nearly thirty major radio ministries, publishers, and other Christian organizations. In 1997, Al was inducted into the National Religious Broadcasters Hall of Fame.

Al lives with his wife, Margaret, in Sunriver, Oregon, and they have three children and six grandchildren.